MW01092723

SUPER CHEAP HOKKAIDO

The Ultimate Budget Travel Guide to Sapporo and
the Hokkaido Prefecture

Matthew Baxter

Help spread the word!

Please help the book by writing a review on the website where you bought the book, sharing the book on Facebook, Twitter or Instagram, or telling a friend. As this is a self-funded indie project, it would be super useful and very much appreciated! It will also allow me to continue to write more budget travel books about this amazing country. Doumo arigatou!

Like or follow us to get the latest tips and deals

Join or follow Super Cheap Guides to get the latest information on new discounts, deals and cherry blossom forecasts, plus interesting budget travel reports. You can also head to our website to read all the latest information or get it sent straight to your inbox by joining the newsletter.

Website: https://www.supercheapguides.com/
Facebook: facebook.com/supercheapguides
Instagram: @SuperCheapGuides
Twitter: @SuperCheapGuide

Super Cheap Guides
9 Eashing Lane
Godalming, Surrey GU7 2JZ
www.supercheapguides.com/contact/

Book Layout ©2019 BookDesignTemplates.com

Ordering Information:
Special discounts are available on quantity purchases by corporations, associations, and others. For details, contact the "Special Sales Department" at the address above.

Super Cheap Hokkaido: The Ultimate Budget Travel Guide to Sapporo and the Hokkaido Prefecture/ Matthew Baxter - 1st ed.
Paperback ISBN 978-1-913114-00-8
Ebook ISBN 978-1-913114-01-5

Contents

i

Welcome to Hokkaido

The beautiful flower fields of Furano in central Hokkaido

Welcome to Hokkaido, Japan's northern island, just waiting to be discovered by the masses. It's a quieter, more spacious and most importantly cheaper place to visit than the rest of Japan, and is full of unspoiled mountains to hike, hot springs to relax in and plenty of local delicacies to enjoy. From historical cities such as Hakodate, to huge ski resorts such as Niseko, to the beautiful flower fields of Furano, Hokkaido really stands out from the rest of Japan. With this guide, you'll find out how to really enjoy it on a reasonable budget.

Compared to the rest of Japan, especially Tokyo and Kyoto, visitors can find some unbelievable prices in Hokkaido. While hostel rooms are often around $30 in Tokyo, don't be surprised to be paying half that in rural Hokkaido. The island still has cheap convenience stores, supermarkets and chain restaurants, it's just that when traveling around you may be a little further away from them than if you were in the big cities down south. Guesthouse owners and locals also appreciate more that visitors from abroad have made the effort to come up to the north too, so don't be surprised to get a random free tour from a local!

The geography and less developed transportation infrastructure can make traveling here challenging at times. This book has been designed so you can see the top sights, as well as experience off-the-beaten-track spots, and all in an affordable and stress-free way.

A little bit of history

Up until the 15th century, Hokkaido was mainly populated by the aboriginal Ainu people, who had their own unique culture, language and traditions, some of which can still be seen today. It's highly recommended to visit towns such as Abashiri to see the Ainu culture in person and to see what makes Hokkaido unique from the rest of Japan. There has also been a surprising amount of western influences over the years, such as the westerners who founded Hokkaido University in Sapporo. Hokkaido did change a lot as mainlanders came over nearly 1000 years ago and forced their customs on the Ainu, with much of Hokkaido's traditions lost or faded, but there is now a concerted effort to protect and display these for tourists and locals alike.

How to save on your holiday with this book

Things to do

With this book you'll be shown plenty of options for free things to do, as well as information on available discounts or places to try free samples. Try to do the cheaper or free activities first, then if you feel you need to do more, try the more expensive things in the area. For example, you may find after doing a free walk somewhere that taking that expensive ropeway up another mountain for a hike isn't worth it.

Sample itineraries and discount passes

While Hokkaido has a smaller number of tourist spots to choose from than the rest of Japan, planning a trip can be difficult because of the infrequent bus or train routes. If you are a bit stuck, use the sample itineraries in this book to help you out.

Budget food

Hokkaido does have budget restaurant chains in the big cities, but you are just as likely to enter a cheap family-owned joint here. These are included on the maps, as well as in the Budget Food sections, as they can be tricky to find if you're not a local. Don't forget to consider buying food from supermarkets or convenience stores, especially if in a tourist town populated mainly with expensive restaurants.

   Most of the budget restaurants have water jugs to refill your bottle. The 100-yen shops (around $1) are also listed, as you can buy almost anything, from microwavable curry to essential travel items. Japanese pharmacies and drugstores often have even cheaper prices for drinks and snacks as well. Tap water is drinkable.

How to use the maps

For hard to navigate towns, maps are provided to help you get around, with handy icons to show you exactly where all the cheap shops, restaurants and more are located. Landmark buildings and major hotels have also been included to aid in navigating around. A plus is that most of these landmarks have toilets if needed, plus many have free water fountains, which can be used to refill your water bottle and save on the cost of drinks. You can also save on transportation by using the recommended walking routes.

Map Legend

 Convenience store   Tourist information   Parking

 Cheap supermarket   Recommended walking route   Post office

 100-yen store   Budget accommodation   Drugstore

Free wifi locations

There is free wifi in many tourist spots and at most tourist information centers in Hokkaido, but there may be slim pickings elsewhere. If you feel you will definitely need the internet at all times, get yourself a data SIM card at the airport or a large electronics store (such as Yodobashi Camera in Sapporo), with prices starting at around 4000 yen a week.

Map of Hokkaido

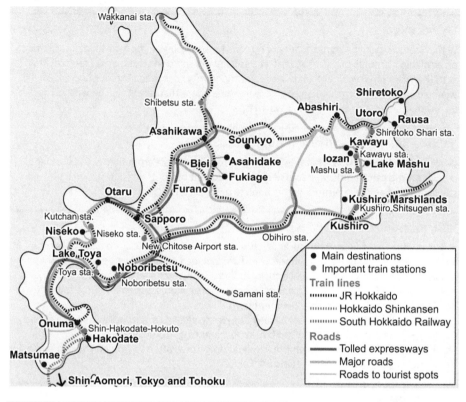

Wakkanai sta.

Shibetsu sta.

Shiretoko
Abashiri Utoro
Asahikawa Rausa
Sounkyo Shiretoko Shari sta.
Kawayu
Biei Asahidake Iozan Kawayu sta.
Fukiage Lake Mashu
Mashu sta.
Otaru Furano
Kutchan sta. Sapporo Kushiro Marshlands
Niseko Niseko sta. Kushiro Shitsugen sta.
Lake Toya New Chitose Airport sta. Kushiro
Toya sta. Noboribetsu Obihiro sta.
Noboribetsu sta.
Samani sta.
Onuma
Shin-Hakodate-Hokuto
Matsumae Hakodate

↓ Shin-Aomori, Tokyo and Tohoku

- Main destinations
- Important train stations

Train lines
.... JR Hokkaido
.... Hokkaido Shinkansen
.... South Hokkaido Railway

Roads
—— Tolled expressways
===== Major roads
—— Roads to tourist spots

Hokkaido Top Five Spots

1) Otaru
Beautiful canal town not far from Sapporo. Great any time of the year, it's a lovely place to take a stroll, trying out the odd local snacks along the way and taking in the fresh coastal air.

2) Hakodate
This large port city has Japan's most famous fish market, one of the country's best night views and a fascinating history. There are also plenty of festivals to enjoy here.

3) Furano
The flower capital of Japan, tourists flock here from all over the world to see the famous multi-colored lavender fields. They love the stuff here, offering lavender ice cream, cosmetics and anything else that can be enriched with the stuff!

4) Toyako Onsen
Many years ago the volcano erupted near Lake Toya, leaving much of the area as a ghost town. You can explore this eerie spot, as well as take a cruise or bike around the peaceful lake.

5) Noboribetsu Onsen
A very atmospheric hot spring town. There are a bunch of free activities to do here, from hiking to foot baths, plus one of the few hot springs where you can drink a beer while bathing!

When to go to Hokkaido

Hokkaido's mild summer and awesome snow are big draws. Just remember to check that places you want to visit are open and transportation is in operation when you want to visit, as things can open on a seasonal basis here. Be sure to check www.supercheapguides.com for this year's timings for cherry blossoms and autumn leaves.

Spring (March to May)
A great time to visit, as tourist spots start to open again for warmer weather, though it should be noted that Hokkaido can still be very chilly in early spring. Due to this colder climate, cherry blossoms bloom a little later and there can still be snow during March, especially in the north.

Summer (June to August)
Get away from the humidity that attacks the rest of Japan in Hokkaido's mild summer climate. The snow should all be gone by now, so there are plenty of free or cheap outdoor activities on offer such as hiking, plus you'll be able to get away from the large crowds in Tokyo or Osaka.

Fall/Autumn (September to November)
The autumn colors are out, so it's an even better time to come out for a hike or city walk. The top spots for autumn leaves viewing will also be much quieter than in Tokyo. It can start to get cold in the evenings, so be sure to bring a good coat.

Winter (December to February)
Countless amazing winter festivals, winter sports such as snowboarding and skiing, boat rides through a sea of ice; winter in Hokkaido is pretty mind-blowing. It's also super cold, so bring lots of warm clothing and confirm the safety of roads at your hostel/hotel before driving.

Peak seasons to avoid
Try to avoid Golden Week (April 29th to May 5th), Obon holidays (around August 13th to 16th) and around the New Year holidays, when prices can go up a little. Unless you are coming for the festival, avoid Sapporo during the extremely busy Sapporo Snow Festival.

Free festivals in Hokkaido

January
Around January 25th to mid-March Sounkyo Hot Springs Ice Festival: A little ice kingdom is created in this hot spring town every year, with brightly lit up igloos, a 100 meter ice tunnel, an 'ice shrine', fireworks and attractions for the children to enjoy.

February
Early to mid-February Sapporo Snow Festival: One of Japan's biggest festivals, featuring some super huge snow and ice sculptures, as well as fun winter activities and games. Book accommodation as early as you can. See the Sapporo chapter for more information.
Early to mid-February Asahikawa Winter Festival: While certainly not as grand as the Sapporo Snow Festival, there are still some amazing sculptures and a cool fireworks display. Come here if you can't find a cheap room for the Sapporo festival.
Starts second week of February (10 days) Otaru Snow Light Path Festival: Also worthwhile visiting in mid-February, this festival sees snowy Otaru's famous canal lit up at night with thousands of small candles in mini glass floats.

March
Early March Kalulus Onsen Winter Festival, Noboribetsu: Winter fun and games at Sanraiba Ski Hill, plus some hearty winter food to warm you up.

Sapporo Snow Festival

April
The cherry blossom season starts in late April. See the cherry blossoms guide in this book.

May
Early May to early June Shibazakura Festival, Takinoue: Acres of park and hillside filled with pink and white moss phloxes, it's a truly beautiful sight and very photogenic. Takinoue is to the east of New Chitose Airport and on the way to Obihiro station.

June
Around June 14th-16th Hokkaido Shrine Festival, Sapporo: Enjoy lots of cheap festival food and see some traditional ceremonies at Sapporo's main shrine. The final day sees thousands parade in colorful Heian period costumes, alongside the shrine's floats and portable shrines.

July
First weekend Yakumo Andon Fireworks: Celebrating children and youth, this lively festival is another one of Hokkaido's biggies. Big floats, Japanese dancing and cheap festival food, it's got it all. Yakumo is one hour north of Onuma by car, or north on the train (90 mins, 2350 yen).
Around July 20th-August 15th Sapporo Odori Beer Garden: A huge beer garden takes over Odori Park, with thousands of people enjoying local and international beers.
Last weekend of July Furano Bellybutton Festival (Hokkai Heso Matsuri): It's time for something a little bit different with this one. Over 5000 people come to dance and turn their bellybuttons into faces, with funny costumes, make-up and other props.
Fourth Friday and Saturday Shiretoko Shari Neputa, Shari: 15 illuminated 'Neputa' floats, some up to eight meters high, are paraded in the center of Shari town.

August
Mid-August Kachimai Fireworks Festival, Obihiro: The biggest fireworks festival in Hokkaido, with 20,000 plus shooting their way into the sky. Takes place at Tokachigawa Park, a short bus or car ride from Obihiro station.
Late August Yotaka Andon Festival, Numata: See this small city come to life, with a huge Japanese float parade and some awesome Taiko drum performances. Located outside Ishikari-Numata station, near Asahikawa (50 mins from Asahikawa station, 930 yen).

September
Mid to late September Sapporo Autumn Festival: The 2 km-long Odori Park in central Sapporo is taken over by massive food courts, serving food that makes the city so famous, such as butter miso ramen. There is also food from across the world, as well as lots and lots of beer!

October
Mid-late October Akanko Marimo Festival, Lake Akan: A marimo is a sphere-shaped alga unique to Lake Akan and a designated natural treasure. See the ancient rituals of the native Ainu people, including traditional dances and torch marches around the marimo.

November
Late Nov to late Dec Sapporo White Illumination: Odori Park gets beautifully lit up for winter.

December
December 1st-25th Hakodate Christmas Fantasy: A traditional Christmas celebration, with a large Christmas tree on the waterfront, fireworks and classic Christmas decorations.

Cherry blossom viewing (花見)

Cherry blossom trees engulfing Fort Goryokaku in Hakodate

As Hokkaido is a sparsely populated prefecture, it can be a rather peaceful way to enjoy the cherry blossoms. Many people head out into the mountains or drive down scenic roads to enjoy Hokkaido during this season. Due to the colder climate, Hokkaido has its cherry blossom season a little later than other prefectures. The first bloom is usually late April, with full bloom in early May. Check the latest forecasts at www.supercheapguides.com before you go.

Top 5 spots for cherry blossoms

1) Fort Goryokaku (Hakodate)
A very popular destination any time of the year, get more bang for your buck by visiting in the spring. Features more than 1000 cherry blossom trees, which have rare pale flowers.

2) Hakodate Park
This free park is another good spot to visit. Visitors can also enjoy a beer and cheap food from local food stalls while relaxing under the pink trees. Also popular is coming at night, when the trees are lit up.

3) Noboribetsu Onsen Flower Tunnel

Located on the road up to this famous hot spring, the 'Flower Tunnel' starts from the Noboribetsu Higashi Interchange. The stunning cherry blossoms continue for more than eight kilometers. On a clear blue sky day, you'll probably get the best pictures of your trip.

4) Odori Park (Sapporo)

This centrally located park is super easy to get to. While it can get far more crowded than others in Hokkaido, the countless cheap beers and Japanese foods on offer definitely make up for it. Later, if you need even more cherry blossom action when in Sapporo, also be sure to check out Maruyama Park and Moerenuma Park.

5) Asahiyama Park (Asahikawa)

Another free park, this one should have lots of space to sit down and chill out in. Asahiyama Park has more than 3000 cherry blossom trees, many of which are lit up at night.

Tax-free shopping

Japan has a sales tax of 8%, but those with a tourist visa are eligible for tax-free shopping. Almost every shop in areas frequented by tourists will offer tax-free shopping in Hokkaido.

How to do tax-free shopping in Japan

All you need to do in the shop is show your passport and the tax will be taken off when you purchase. Some naughty shops levy a charge to get tax-free, so avoid these if it's mentioned. All the shops included in this book should offer tax-free shopping.

Consumables (foods, drinks, medicines, cosmetics…)
Must be purchased at the same store on the same day, and the total spending must be more than 5000 yen. Items must be taken out of Japan within 30 days of purchase.

Non-consumables (electric appliances, clothing, accessories…)
Must be purchased at the same store on the same day, and the total spending must be more than 5000 yen. Items must be taken out of Japan within six months of purchase.

Getting to and around Hokkaido

How to get there and away

By air

Flying to New Chitose Airport near Sapporo provides the greatest number of budget flight options, but Hakodate Airport also has a few budget airlines that fly there. Vanilla Air, Jetstar and Peach are the best for cheap domestic flights.

Airport transportation
From New Chitose Airport to Sapporo, take the Airport train (40 mins, 1070 yen). Hakodate Airport has a shuttle bus (20 mins, 450 yen) or the slower route 96 bus (33 mins, 290 yen) heading to/from Hakodate station.

By train

If you have a rail pass, you can get to Hokkaido from Tokyo on the Hokkaido Shinkansen (bullet train). Otherwise, taking the train to Hokkaido is very pricey and takes far more time than a quick budget flight from cities such as Tokyo or Osaka.

Getting around by car or motorbike

As the trains are infrequent in many areas of Hokkaido, travelers should definitely consider using a car or motorbike. Signs are all in English, roads are well paved and most rental companies give out GPS units as standard, so it's not too difficult to get around. Use the Mapcode or telephone numbers in this guide to find your way by entering them in your GPS. The best period to drive is May to October, as snowy and icy conditions in winter can hamper drivers. Note that while most towns have a gas station, they can close in the early evening.

If you need a short rest on your journey, it's a good idea to stop at a 'Michi-no-eki' (roadside station). As well as cheap restaurants and a shop showing off local goods, there is 24-hour parking, an ATM, tourist information, road condition update boards and toilets. Ones on the roads between places in this book are mentioned in the relevant chapters, but if you need to see more head to https://www.michi-no-eki.jp/stations/english.

There are campsites across Hokkaido, but few take reservations in English, either online or on the phone. If you plan to stay at a campsite, you could check availability at a tourist information center or ask them to find and book your next campsite for you. It might also be a good idea to get your previous accommodation to do this if you don't speak Japanese.

Hokkaido Expressway Pass

Using the expressways isn't essential, especially on a budget, but can be useful if you are short for time on your Hokkaido holiday. Use Google Maps to see if it's worth it for your plans. If you do decide so, tourists are recommended to get the Hokkaido Expressway Pass. It allows for unlimited use of the expressways, cutting out a lot of hassle and potentially saving a lot. Available from car rental companies. *From 807 to 1800 yen per day (2 to 14 days)*

Sample itineraries

Sapporo to Kushiro (7-8 days)
Start by picking up your car at New Chitose Airport near Sapporo, then head to Furano for some skiing or the flower fields, depending on the season. Next drive to Sounkyo Onsen for some mountain hiking or the ice festival, before continuing to Abashiri if it's winter for the ice cruises, or to World Heritage Shiretoko Park if in summer. Finally, proceed south via the mystical Lake Mashu, ending up at Kushiro to reward yourself with some super fresh seafood.

South Hokkaido to Sapporo (6-7 days)
After a day taking in the history of port city Hakodate, pick up your car and head down for a day in Matsumae to see Hokkaido's only traditional Japanese castle. Next, continue around to Onuma to stretch your legs with a walk in the forest. From here, head for the hot springs, hiking and more in Toyako Onsen and Noboribetsu. Finally continue to Sapporo, or New Chitose Airport if that's the end of your trip.

Getting around on the train

Hokkaido has a much less developed and convenient train network than the rest of Japan, but it's still perfectly possible with a little patience and the odd use of local buses to fill the gaps. Just be sure to check that there will be a train back at the end of the day.

Getting around by bus

If you would prefer not to drive and the train times are not convenient for you, it may be worth checking the bus routes. Bus networks aren't as good as in other prefectures, so be sure to pre-book or get help from your hostel if booking when you're in Japan. If you need to use many buses, it may be worth getting a Budget Bus Pass at www.budget-buspass.com.

Discount transportation passes and tickets

JAL Japan Explorer Pass and the ANA Experience Japan Fare
Japan Airlines and ANA offer special discount tickets for foreign travelers. You'll be able to get flights to Hokkaido from other prefectures for just 10,800 yen and internal flights for a crazily low price of 5400 yen. Note that there are a limited number of these tickets, so book fast!

JR Hokkaido Rail Pass
Allows unlimited use of all JR trains, except the Hokkaido Shinkansen (bullet train), in Hokkaido. As you'll need to travel on fast 'Limited Express' trains to cover the large distances on the island, train ticket costs could really mount up if you don't use such a pass. Only for those with tourist visas, it can be bought from overseas travel agents or at large stations like Sapporo, Hakodate or New Chitose Airport. If you are also traveling elsewhere in Japan and would like to travel via the Shinkansen, then consider the national Japan Rail Pass. *3 days: Adults 16,500 yen, children 8,250 yen. Flexible (non-consecutive days) 4 days: Adults 22,000 yen, children 11,000 yen. 5 days: Adults 22,000 yen, children 11,000 yen. 7 days: Adults 24,000 yen, children 12,000 yen*

JR Tohoku-South Hokkaido Rail and East-South Hokkaido Rail passes
If you are also visiting places such as Sendai down south, the Tohoku-South Hokkaido pass might be worth it. It provides unlimited use of JR trains, including the Shinkansen, and can take you as far as Sapporo and Otaru in southern Hokkaido. One plus is that the five days in the pass are flexible, meaning you can use it non-consecutively over a two week period. If you also want to include Tokyo, get the flexible six day East-South Hokkaido pass instead. Buy both outside Japan, as they are 1000 yen more to buy in Japan. *Tohoku-South Hokkaido Rail Pass: Adults 19,000 yen, children 9,500 yen. East-South Hokkaido Rail Pass: Adults 26,000 yen, children 13,000 yen*

Other JR Hokkaido discount tickets
If you are flying with Peach, Vanilla Air or AirDo, depending on where you arrive in Hokkaido you may be able to use passes exclusive to passengers of these airlines. Check http://www2.jrhokkaido.co.jp/global/english/ticket/otoku/index.html for the latest offers.

Sample itineraries

Hokkaido summer highlights (JR Hokkaido Rail Pass, 4-6 days)
After a day or two exploring the history of Hokkaido's capital Sapporo, make your way west to Otaru. Spend a night here so you can have a walk along the canal and enjoy the local food at night before heading back. Next make your way to Furano and Biei, giving yourself two days to explore the lavender fields in good time. Those that enjoy hiking should add on some time up the spectacular Mount Asahidake, or if you are with the kids head to the superb Asahikawa Zoo. If you have time, continue down to Hakodate after this.

Sapporo to Hakodate (Any JR pass, 6-8 days)
From Sapporo, or from New Chitose Airport, head to the hot spring town of Noboribetsu Onsen to relax after your flight for a night or two, as well as seeing some huge monster statues on your walks around this classic resort town. Next, continue west to Toyako Onsen to see what a town looks like after a volcanic eruption, then after a night here head down to Hakodate, breaking up the long journey at Onuma for some light hiking. Once in Hakodate you can enjoy the fish market and the fascinating history of this port city.

Out in the sticks (JR Hokkaido Rail Pass, 7 days)
Start at Kushiro Airport or New Chitose Airport (if you want to visit Furano for the lavender fields before heading east to Kushiro). At Kushiro you can see the marshlands and local nature on the awesome tourist train. Next head north to Lake Mashu for a few days to see the

pristine scenery as well as experience some nearby volcanic action. Finally head to the small port town of Abashiri or continue all the way back to Sapporo.

Things to know before you visit Hokkaido

Things can definitely be cheaper here than the rest of Japan. Accommodation in particular is sometimes unbelievably low-cost and food can be a little cheaper.

Exchange rates
These are the rates as of February 2019. See www.supercheapguides.com for the latest rates. 1 US Dollar = 110 yen • 1 Euro = 124 yen • 1 British Pound = 142 yen • 1 Canadian Dollar = 83 yen • 1 Australian Dollar = 78 yen

Average daily costs for budget travelers
Single Traveler: 5000-7000 yen • Multiple travelers: 3000-5000 yen per person

Usual prices
Dorm bed: 1500-3500 yen • Budget eat-in meal: 390-600 yen • Convenience store meal: 290-500 yen • Cup noodles: 100-190 yen • Subway ticket: 165-195 yen

Money
Especially outside of Sapporo, it is essential to have cash with you at all times. Hardly any restaurants or shops will accept credit cards, so make sure you get enough money from an ATM. 7-Eleven are your best choice for an ATM, but most convenience store ATMs will accept foreign cards these days. As with the rest of Japan, tipping is a real no-no, which is nice.

Electricity
Hokkaido has an electrical current of 100v, 50Hz. Visitors from Europe will probably need to get an adapter, but those from North America may sometimes be fine as the shapes of the pins are identical. You can buy a cheap adapter at the airport or in large electronics stores.

Visas
Japan allows visa free travel from most countries for tourists, but make sure you check with your Japanese embassy. If you are interested in working in a farm or ski resort in Hokkaido's countryside, consider getting a working holiday visa if they are available for your nationality.

Coin lockers (コインロッカー)
The subway stations in Sapporo all have lockers. Note that once you get out of the big city only the major train stations like Hakodate or Asahikawa will have them.

Best free apps to download before you go

- Skyscanner for comparing cheap airplane tickets.
- Google Translate, then download the Japanese language pack in the app for offline use. Also translates text with your phone camera. Great when trying to decipher Japanese menus!
- Japan Connected-Free Wifi, to easily find free wifi spots.
- Booking.com to quickly cancel or amend bookings. Airbnb is also worth downloading.
- Google Maps and Maps.me, then in Maps.me download the areas you will be visiting.
- XE Currency for comparing prices to back home.
- Splittr, which allows you to see who owes what to who when traveling with friends.
- Japan Transit Planner (Norikae Annai) by Jorudan for train times. Hyperdia and Japan Bus Online are also excellent websites for travel planning.

Sapporo (札幌)

A flowery welcome from the Former Hokkaido Government Office, Odori Park

The largest city in Hokkaido, Sapporo is quite a new city that only really sprung into life in the 19th century. With an easy-to-navigate, American-style grid system and a deep history of foreign influences, it definitely feels different to other Japanese cities. While the attractions here should not take more than a day or two to enjoy, it's a great place to start your adventures from, especially with all the budget flights to nearby New Chitose Airport.

How to get around Sapporo

Sapporo has a well-developed public transportation system, with subway lines, buses and streetcars able to take you to any tourist spot or neighborhood. There is a local smart card called Sapica, which reduces prices by up to 10% and has a refundable deposit, as well as eliminating any extra charges when transferring. On the other hand, visitors can just use smart cards from other major cities instead, such as Tokyo's Suica card, or Hokkaido's card, Kitaca. Sapica is available from ticket machines at subway stations, while the Kitaca cards can be found in JR stations. *Both cards 2000 yen (500 yen deposit, 1500 yen put on card)*

Discount passes and tickets

One-Day Ticket for Subway Use
Allows unlimited rides on the subway system for a whole day. Subway fares start from 200 yen, so you'll easily save a few hundred yen using this pass. Buy from any subway station ticket machine. There is also a cheaper pass, called the Donichika Ticket, available on Saturdays, Sundays, national holidays and New Year holidays. *Adults 830 yen, children 420 yen. Donichika Ticket: Adults 520 yen, children 260 yen*

Dosanko Pass

If you are staying on the streetcar line or plan to use it often, consider this pass. It allows unlimited use of the streetcars for a whole day for 1 adult and 1 child. As tickets cost from 170 one way, it's a great deal for families. Note that it's only available on weekends, national holidays and New Year holidays. Buy on the streetcar. *1 Adult + 1 Child 360 yen (combined ticket)*

Common-Use One-Day Card

Allows unlimited use of the subway, streetcars as well as city buses for a whole day. If you plan to pack in a lot in one day and need more than one mode of public transportation, it's a no brainer. Available to buy at any subway station. *Adults 1000 yen, children 500 yen.*

'Sapporo Walk' Sapporo Beer Garden and Factory Line (Loop Bus route 88)

Some attractions are a little away from any subway station. This loop bus takes visitors to the Sapporo Beer Garden, the Bus Center, Odori Park, Sapporo Clock Tower and Sapporo Station. *Adults 210 yen, children 100 yen. One-day pass: Adults 750 yen, children 380 yen*

Sapporo transportation map

There is usually more than one way to get anywhere in Sapporo. Use this map below to help you get around. Note that, for ease of reading, this map only includes major stations.

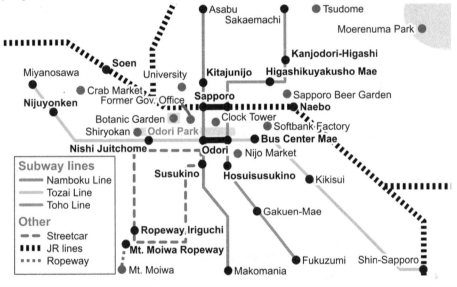

Things to do

Central Sapporo

Sapporo Beer Garden and Museum (サッポロ ビール園)

If you are into your beer, this place is a must. Located in red brick buildings built more than 100 years ago, it's now registered as an official Hokkaido Heritage site. The beer museum gives an insightful look at the history and science of beer in Japan, such as displays of old fashioned posters used to introduce beer to Japan. Afterwards, guests can try out an exclusive selection of beers, as well as some old favorites. *FREE entry and self-guided tour (beers from 300 yen) • 11am-8pm (last order 6:30pm) • By subway: 10 mins walk from Higashikuyakusho-Mae station. By JR train: 10 mins walk from Naebo station. By bus: Take the Loop Bus 88 (210 yen) • Tel: 011-748-1876*

14

Entrance to Sapporo Beer Museum

Former Hokkaido Government Office (北海道庁旧本庁舎)
Also known as the Red Brick Office, this building was built in 1888 and is a stunning example of foreign influenced architecture. Inside there are lots of little exhibitions to check out, as well as a short introduction to the history and politics of Hokkaido. The gift shop also has some amusing, Hokkaido-themed presents. *FREE • 8:45am-6pm • Between Sapporo and Odori stations*

Botanic Garden (植物園)
Another good place to pass the time in Sapporo. Split into many different sections with around 4000 species in total, it's a relaxing respite from the rest of the city. *Adults 420 yen, children 300 yen, under 6 FREE • 9am-4:30pm (April to September), 9am-4pm (October to November 3rd) (closed Mondays) • 10 minute walk from Sapporo station or Odori Park*

JR Tower (JR タワー)
The T38 Observation Deck is not an essential visit, but if you want to get a view over the city then this is the best option. *Adults 720 yen, children 300-500 yen • 10am-11pm • In Sapporo station*

University grounds (北海道大学)
The public is welcome to enter the large university grounds, which features a selection of 19th century buildings and statues commemorating the university's western founders. *FREE • 24h • 10 minute walk from Sapporo station or just outside Kitajunijo subway station*

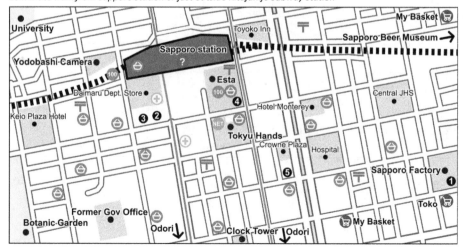

Odori Park (大通公園) and south Sapporo

Often lined with beer gardens and sculptures, Odori Park is a worthwhile place to visit almost any day of the year. It takes about 20 minutes to walk from one side to another.

Clock Tower (札幌市時計台)

A symbol of Hokkaido, this building is a great place to enter if you want to know about the influence the west made on Hokkaido. Built way back in 1878, it uses a grand clock brought over from Boston. The site is not too big, but if you are not interested in history, it's best just to take some photos from outside and save on the entrance fee! *Adults 200 yen, children FREE • 8:45am-5pm (closed on New Year's day) • 10 minutes on foot from Odori station or Sapporo station*

Shiryokan (札幌市資料館)

The former Sapporo Court of Appeals is another free place to check out for those interested in art and culture in Hokkaido. It's not too detailed, but if you have time it may be worth checking out. They also often have fun activities for kids to participate in as well. *FREE • 9am-7pm (closed Mondays) • Located on west end of Odori Park*

Nijo Fish Market (二条市場)

Although not as big and impressive as Hakodate's fish markets, it's worth having a stroll around this market, seeing the locals at work and discovering all the strange fish on offer. *FREE • 7am-6pm • 10 minute walk from Odori station*

Susukino (すすきの)

Sapporo's red light district. The shopping arcades right around Susukino station are not as sleazy and have loads of shops and restaurants to explore, with tax-free options galore.

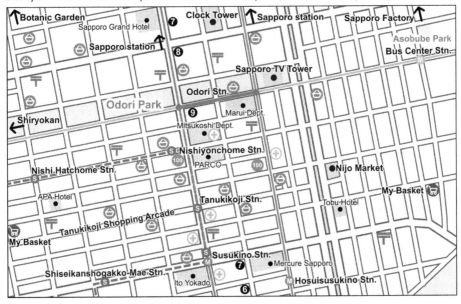

Outer Sapporo

Moerenuma Park (モエレ沼公園)

Quite a surprisingly innovative mixture of modern art and architecture, designed by sculptor Isamu Noguchi, who wanted to create a place where art and nature come together. Has a playground for the kids and also provides a decent view over the city. *FREE • 7am-10pm • Take the Toho Line to Kanjodori-Higashi station, then get bus no. 69 or 79 with Chuo Bus and get off at 'Moerenuma koen higashiguchi' (25 mins, 210 yen) • Mapcode: 9 741 565*47*

Sapporo Central Wholesale Market (札幌場外市場)

More than 60 stores packed together, selling fresh fish, seafoods and other traditional Hokkaido produce. Prices are reasonably cheap and some stores can cook the food for you, right there and then. *FREE • 9am-3pm (closed Sundays) • Either take the JR train to Soen station from Sapporo (3 mins, 170 yen) or the subway from Odori station to Nijuyonken station (10 minutes, 250 yen). The market is a 10 minute walk from either station (on North 11, West 21) • Tel: 011 621 7044 • Mapcode: 9 549 090*60*

Mount Moiwa (藻岩山)

This forest-covered mountain makes for a great day trip. The view from the top is said to be one of Japan's three best night views, with the observation deck providing spectacular views over the city lights. There are various options for getting to the top:

Hike up Mount Moiwa

Hiking up is a great way to save on the pricey ropeway and explore the forests. Routes can be reasonably busy, but at least this means you can't get lost! There is a trailhead at the base of Moiwa Ski Resort, from where a 2.5km hiking route takes you to the summit. The start point is a short walk before the resort entrance, so just look out for the hiking map or follow other hikers. You can hike up and take the ropeway down, or vice versa, for about half the price. *Difficulty: Easy • Time required: about 80 minutes • From Sapporo station's bus terminal, take the Jyotetsu 'South 55 Moiwa Line' bus (25 minutes, 200 yen) to South 34, West 11 (show 南34 条西11 丁目 to the bus driver to be sure), which is a short walk from the start • Mapcode: 9 340 167*25 (hiking start point)*

Mount Moiwa Ropeway and Cable Car

The ropeway up gives stunning, unobstructed views via its large glass walls. The cable car then takes visitors through a serene forest to the top, but feel free to skip this to save on costs, as it's a short walk instead. *Ropeway + cable car: Adults 1700 yen, children 850 yen. Ropeway only: Adults 1100, children 550 yen • 10:30am-10pm (summer), 11am-10pm (winter) • Take the streetcar from Susukino to Ropeway Iriguchi (22 mins, 200 yen), which is near the ropeway • Mapcode: 9 400 432*00*

By car on the Mount Moiwa toll road

If you have a car, you can also drive up to the car park at the top via a toll road. *660 yen • 10:30am-10pm (closed December to mid-April) • Mapcode: 9 369 344*88 (summit)*

Sapporo Snow Festival (さっぽろ雪まつり)

The biggest and best festival in Hokkaido, if not Japan. A huge number of snow and ice sculptures are put on display, with everything from the Taj Mahal to Pokemon characters, at heights of up to 25 meters. The festival is located at Odori Park, Susukino and the further out Tsudome, which has lots of facilities for families, such as snow slides and snow rafting. *FREE entry • Early February (see http://www.snowfes.com/english/ for the next festivals exact dates and events) • Tsudome is a 15-minute walk or short shuttle bus ride (100 yen) from Sakaemachi station on the Toho Line. There are also shuttle buses from Sapporo station and Odori Park (210 yen)*

Volunteer guides and tours

The local Chamber of Commerce Sightseeing Volunteer Guide group runs free tours, such as a walk of the center. At least two people are required for a tour to go ahead, and reservations are required. See http://www.sight-de.com/guide/ or email intl@sapporo-cci.or.jp.

Budget food

Central Sapporo

1) Tonyoshi (とんよし) - Pork cutlet meals. *Lunch sets 820 yen • 11am-2am • Sapporo Factory*
2) Yoshinoya (吉野家) - Gyudon (pork on rice) eat-in and takeaway. *Meals from 330 yen • 24h • In the underground shopping mall on the south side of Sapporo station*

3) Curry Club Ono - Cheap Japanese curry. *Meals from 600 yen • 10:30am-10pm • Near to Yoshinoya*

4) Mos Burger (モス) - Cheap Japanese burger chain. *From 220 yen • 10am-9pm • Esta mall*

5) Yayoiken (やよい軒) - Traditional Japanese set dishes, with free rice and tea refills. *Meals from 650 yen • 10am-12:30am • Short walk from Sapporo subway exit 22*

Delicious Sapporo butter miso ramen from the Ramen Yokocho

Odori and Susukino

6) Ramen Yokocho (ラーメン横丁) - Collection of noodle bars, some specializing in Sapporo's famous butter miso ramen. *Bowls from around 600-800 yen • Various times • Near Susukino station*

7) Matsuya (松屋) - Gyudon and burger eat-in and takeaway. *Gyudon bowls from 290 yen • 24h • Just outside exit 9 of Odori station and also near Susukino station*

8) Sukiya (すき家) - Curry and gyudon. *From 360 yen • 24h • Just outside exit 11 of Odori station*

9) Bikkuri Donkey (びっくりドンキー) - Family favorites at reasonable prices. *Meals from 750 yen • 9am-9pm • Just outside Odori station exit 15*

Cheap supermarkets (スーパー)

There are a few MyBasket minimarts (24h), which although having a small range, have dirt cheap prices. Toko (9am-11pm), next to Sapporo Factory, has a much larger range.

Shopping

Sapporo Factory (サッポロファクトリー) - If you want to do a bit of tax-free shopping, come to this mega mall. *10am-10pm • 15 minute walk from Sapporo station*

Esta (札幌エスタ) - Tax-free options galore: Uniqlo and GU for cheap clothes, Bic Camera for electronics, ABC Mart for shoes and so much more. *10am-9pm • Outside Sapporo station*

Tokyu Hands (東急ハンズ) - Huge variety store. *10am-8pm • Opposite Esta*

Yodobashi (ヨドバシカメラ) - Big tax-free electronics store. *10am-10pm • Near Sapporo station*

100-yen shops

Seria (セリア) - In 4Chome Plaza (Odori station, exit 10) and Sapporo Factory. *10am-8:30pm*

Daiso (ダイソー) - Has a branch conveniently located outside Sapporo station. *10am-9pm*

CanDo (キャンドゥ) - In Esta, and Ario Sapporo, next to the Sapporo Beer Museum. *9am-9pm*

Drugstores (ドラッグ ストア)

There are many around town, most open late. See the maps for the locations.

Recommended cheap accommodation

The Stay Sapporo Nagomi
Newly furnished, friendly hostel with new dormitory rooms. *Dorm beds from 3000 yen • Near Susukino •* http://thestay.jp/sapporo-nagomi/ *• Tel: 011-222-0753*

Sapporo International Youth Hostel (札幌 国際 ユース ホステル)
Another reliable hostel, this one has more room types and is in a quieter location. *Beds from 2700 yen • Near Gakuen-Mae subway station •* http://www.youthhostel.or.jp/kokusai/ *• Tel: 011-825-3120*

Hotel Potmum Sapporo (ホテル ポットマム)
More upmarket hostel and hotel, which also has private rooms. *Dorm beds from 3000 yen, private rooms from 8000 yen • Near Kikusui subway station •* https://www.potmumhotel.jp/ *• Tel: 011-826-4500*

Joy Cafe (ジョイ-カフェ)
Internet café with free drinks, comics and cheap food (showers 360 yen extra). *9 hours (9 時間 ナイトパック) from 1519 yen • Across the road from Esta mall, outside Sapporo station*

How to get there and away

By air
From cities outside Hokkaido, it's always cheaper to fly, unless you're using a rail pass. Flights mostly arrive at New Chitose Airport.

By train
Sapporo station has plenty of fast 'Limited Express' trains from most of the main stations, so if you have a rail pass it's easy, if sometimes time consuming, to get the train here. See relevant chapters for times and prices.

By bus
There are buses that go from Sapporo station or the bus center. Buses may be more convenient and cheaper than the trains. See the relevant chapters for more information.

By car
There are plenty of rental car companies to pick up a car from in Sapporo or at New Chitose Airport. To Otaru it takes about 40 minutes and to Noboribetsu it takes about one hour and a half. There are countless parking lots in the city, but most will charge a bit, so if your accommodation has free parking be sure to make use of this.

Mapcode: 9 522 149*25 (city center)

Tourist information

The Hokkaido-Sapporo Tourist Information Center is located in Sapporo station (8:30am-9pm).

West Hokkaido

Otaru (小樽)

A medium-sized city about one hour from Sapporo, Otaru is well known all over Japan for its lovely, quiet canal. While there are plenty of tour buses and touristy shops, Otaru has a really laid-back feel and rarely feels overcrowded. The downtown area is both very walkable and is also full of free attractions, so is a great location for a very cheap return trip from Sapporo or stop-off along the way to Niseko.

Discount pass: Otaru Round Tour Ticket

An option if you don't possess a rail pass already, this ticket provides a return ticket from Sapporo, plus use of the local buses. It will save you money if you are not up for walking around all the time, but otherwise just getting single train tickets would be cheaper. Buy at Sapporo station. If you have kids to entertain, you can also add on entry to Otaru Aquarium. With dolphin shows, penguins and more, it should keep the little ones busy for a bit! (9am-4pm). *Adults: 1940 yen, children 970 yen. Plus Aquarium: Adults: 2540 yen, children 1170-2040 yen*

Things to do

Otaru Canal (小樽運河)
Spectacular any time of the day, but particularly at night when it's lit up, Otaru Canal is a relaxing place to take a stroll. A must-see in Otaru, there are some interesting shops along the canal, so be sure to visit both sides to check out all the tax-free shopping opportunities.

North Canal
Most tourists don't go up here, but there are some interesting old dilapidated canal buildings, such as an old municipal hall and a few interesting cafes. Just walk north up Otaru Canal until the end, which takes 10-15 minutes on foot.

Sakaimachi Street (堺町通り)

The main shopping street in Otaru, with loads of shops for souvenirs and local food or drinks. Many of the shops have free samples, so go inside the interesting ones even if they look a bit pricey and see what's on offer!

Nichigin Street (日銀通り)

A former powerhouse of trade and commerce, this street is full of interesting architecture from the time when it was called the 'Wall Street of the north'. Highlights include the The Bank of Japan Otaru Museum building and the old Hokkaido Bank branch.

Former Temiya Railway (旧国鉄手宮線)

Originally constructed to transport coal and marine material, the Temiya Railway was closed in 1985 due to lack of use. These few sections of the track are all that remain of this railway. It's a cool place to check out and have a walk down on the way to one of the Otaru's highlights.

Nikka Whisky Yoichi Distillery (ニッカウヰスキー 北海道工場 余市蒸溜所)

The Yoichi distillery was built in 1934 at a location known for its clean water and brisk weather, reminiscent of Scotland. The self-guided tour shows off the whiskey making process and the work of founder Taketsuru Masataka, who spent several years in Scotland researching whiskey production. At the end there is a tasting room to enjoy as well! *FREE • 9:15am-5pm (closed New Year's) • Located just outside Yoichi station. Take a train from Otaru (24 mins, 360 yen) • Tel: 0135-23-3131 • Mapcode: 164 635 876*25*

Miyako Shopping Street (小樽都通り商店街)

A bit of a ghost town, with many shops closed or opened at random times by their elderly owners, but there are still the odd grocers or funky little café to be found here.

LAOX Duty Free

Lots of tax-free souvenirs and great products, including locally produced sweets, Japanese clothing and travel essentials. *10am-7pm • Located at the canal*

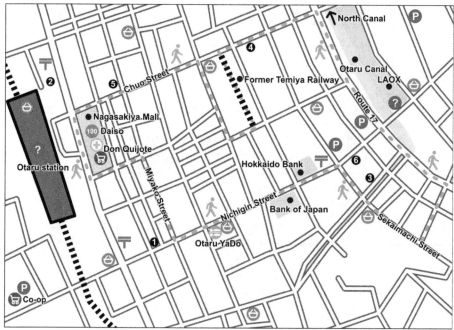

Budget food

1) Mos Burger (モス) - Cheap Japanese burger chain. *Burgers from 220 yen • 9am-11pm*

2) Santaku Market (小樽三角市場) - Small market with plenty of stalls selling fresh produce, and some wonderfully authentic connected takeaways. Try to get here early, as some of the shops can close early if they sell out. *Bowls from around 500-800 yen • 8am-5pm*

3) Kinsho Croquette (金賞コロッケ) - Famous homemade croquette spot, with shaved ice also on offer when it's hot. *Croquette from 180 yen • 9am-6pm*

4) Yamanaka Dairy Farm (山中牧場) - Luxury ice cream using Hokkaido milk, at not too bad a price. *Ice cream from 250 yen • 11am-6pm*

5) Ramen Tokaiya (らーめん渡海家) - Tasty garlic miso ramen with delicious pork toppings. *Ramen from 800 yen • 12am-8:30pm (closed Tuesdays)*

6) Kuwataya (桑田屋) - Sells super cheap 'Panjyu', a ball-shaped muffin baked with bean jam inside. *Panjyu from 89 yen • 9am-9pm • Inside the Otaru Terminal building*

Cheap supermarkets (スーパー)

Co-op Sapporo Midori (9am-10p) is a short drive or 10-minute walk to the west, just outside the center. Nearer the station is Don Quijote, a variety store in Nagasakiya mall (9am-9pm).

100-yen shops

Daiso (ダイソー) - Inside Nagasakiya, just outside the station. *10am-9pm*

Drugstores (ドラッグストア)

Don Quijote (9am-9pm), in Nagasakiya mall, has a large range of goods.

Recommended cheap accommodation

Emina Backpackers (えみな バックパッカーズ)
This small hostel has cheap dorm rooms and a laid-back atmosphere, so great for those on a tight budget. *Dorm beds from 2500 yen, private rooms from 6000 yen • 10 minute drive/bus from Otaru station • https://sites.google.com/view/otaru-emina-backpackers/ • Mapcode: 164 658 896*77*

Otarunai Backpackers' Hostel Morinoki (おたるない バックパッカーズホステル 杜の樹)
More central than Emina, but with just slightly higher prices. *Dorm beds from 3000 yen, private rooms from 7000 yen • Near Sakaimachi Street • https://otaru-backpackers.com/ • Tel: 0134-23-2175*

Otaru YaDo
New hostel with great facilities and various types of rooms to suit most tastes. *Dorm beds from 2000 yen • 10 minute walk from Otaru station • https://www.otaru-yado.jp/ • Tel: 0134-64-7066*

How to get there and away

By train
From Sapporo station, take the train to Otaru station (33 mins, 640 yen).

By car or motorbike
Otaru is about 40 minutes from Sapporo or one hour from Niseko. *Useful Michi-no-eki roadside station: To Niseko, halfway down Route 393 at Mapcode 164 161 744, tel. 0135-34-6699*

Mapcode: 164 719 382*71

Tourist information

There are tourism information centers both in Otaru station and on the canal (9am-6pm).

Niseko (ニセコ)

Looking over Niseko from the top of the Annupuri ski resort

Niseko is by far the most popular ski resort for foreign tourists in Japan, and also the most foreigner-friendly with a host of services and restaurants catering for us. It's therefore a great place to come if this is your first ski or snowboard trip to Japan. Those experienced traveling in Japan may prefer a town like Furano for a less westernized atmosphere. It does though have an impressive collection of resorts, with more than 30 lifts and gondolas, more than 15 meters of snowfall a year and super easy access to the slopes. Before you go, check the latest weather forecasts and snow conditions at http://www.niseko.ne.jp/en/weather/index.html.

Discount pass: Niseko United All Mountain Pass

Save some money and gain access to the four main resorts (about 60% of the total skiing area) for one flat price. Also includes free buses from and back to Kutchan station. The 12 point pass in particular is a great offer, especially if you tend to take your time with the occasional coffee break or meal. *One day pass: Adults 7400 yen, seniors and 13-14 years 5600 yen, 7-12 years 4500 yen. 12-point pass: Adults 4000 yen, seniors and 13-14 years 3600 yen, 7-12 years 3000 yen (riding gondolas costs 4 points, high-speed lifts 2 points, and other lifts 1 point). Reduced one day pass rates are also available if going to Niseko just after or before the peak period (early December to late March): Adults 5100 yen, seniors and 13-14 years 3900 yen, 7-12 years 3100 yen*

Getting around

There is a free bus service called HANAZONO Shuttle Bus that travels around the four main ski resorts and Hirafu village (in operation 7:50am to 5:10pm).

Things to do

Grand Hirafu (グランヒラフ)

The largest ski resort in Niseko, this place has lots of accommodation options and slopes for all levels and interests. Night skiing is also very popular here as it has the greatest number of runs in operation at night, especially as the partner Hanazono Ski Resort is included with passes and tickets. A good choice for newcomers to skiing in Japan.

Full day: Adults 5500 yen, seniors and 13-14 years 4100 yen, 7-12 years 3000 yen
8 hours: Adults 4900 yen, seniors and 13-14 years 3700 yen, 7-12 years 2700 yen
5 hours: Adults 4200 yen, seniors and 13-14 years 3200 yen, 7-12 years 2300 yen
8:30 to 20:30 (late November to early May) • Via HANAZONO Shuttle Bus

Niseko Village (ニセコビレッジ)

Right in the heart of Niseko, this is a good ski resort with some of the steepest slopes for advanced level skiers and snowboarders, as well as some for lower levels. A little more upmarket than others, but it does have the longest skiing and snowboarding trails.

Full day: Adults 5500 yen, seniors and 13-14 years 4200 yen, 7-12 years 3300 yen
Full day (early Dec + late March): Adults 3900 yen, seniors and 13-14 years 2900 yen, 7-12 years 2300 yen
8:30 to 20:00 (early December to early April) • Via HANAZONO Shuttle Bus

Annupuri (ニセコアンヌプリ)

Located at the base of the mountain, Annupuri offers some great powder snow to enjoy and is not as steep as the others. It also has a hot spring to chill out in after and is generally the cheapest of the four resorts to ski or snowboard on (small off season discounts also given). It also has a Nighter pass, allowing super cheap access in the evening.

Full day: Adults 5000 yen, seniors and 13-14 years 3600 yen, 7-12 years 2900 yen
8 hours: Adults 4600 yen, seniors and 13-14 years 3400 yen, 7-12 years 2700 yen
5 hours: Adults 4000 yen, seniors and 13-14 years 2900 yen, 7-12 years 2400 yen
Nighter: 2000 yen • 8:30 to 20:30 (late November to early May) • Via HANAZONO Shuttle Bus

---

Budget food

It's usually best to self-cater via supermarkets to keep costs down as many of the restaurants are quite flashy, but Hirafu Village (also known as Yamada), near the Grand Hirafu resort, has some places to eat out if you don't want to eat at your accommodation. There are also a host of food trucks in the center of town, where you can get a quick meal for under 1000 yen. Here are a few other good options for eating out:

Asahikawa Ramen Tozanken (旭川ラーメン登山軒) - Busy ramen restaurant, serving miso ramen. Also has traditional Japanese set meals. *Ramen from 750 yen • 11am - 10pm • Bus stop J*

BangBang (バンバン) - Yakitori (Japanese meat skewers) and a bunch of other interesting small dishes. *Dishes from 300 yen • 5:30pm-11pm (closed Wednesdays) • Bus stop J*

Cheap supermarkets (スーパー)

Seiko Mart - Open 24 hours, get off at stop B on the HANAZONO Shuttle Bus (located between G and L). There is also a Lawson store nearby.

The Niseko Supermarket & Deli - Open 7am-10pm, this large grocery store is well and truly aimed at the foreign traveler, with English customer service. Near bus stop A.

Co-op - Large supermarket with more reasonable prices, open 9am-9pm, just to the left from Kutchan station.

Hokuyu Lucky - This one probably has the cheapest prices. A few minutes by car from Kutchan station or a 10-minute walk. Open 9:30am-9pm (tel. 0136-21-3677). Also has a 100-yen store! Head down the main road from the station, take the third right and walk to the next block.

100-yen shops

CanDo (キャンドゥ) - Near to Hokuyu Lucky in Kutchan. *9:30am-9pm*

Drugstores (ドラッグストア)

Sapporo Drugstore has a branch (サツドラ) in Hirafu 188 (11am-9pm) near bus stop J.

Water bottle refill spots

Before coming to Niseko, buy yourself a hot water flask in a big city like Sapporo as prices will be considerably higher here, then fill it up at your accommodation.

Recommended cheap accommodation

Even with a family, hostels are usually best here as prices at hotels are often prohibitively expensive. Don't forget to enquire about discounted ski and board rentals when you book.

Karimpani Niseko Fujiyama (ユースホステル カリンパニ・ニセコ藤山)
Large Hostelling International hostel, with dorm and private rooms at good prices. Free wifi and rental services available. A bit out of town, but you can contact them for a pick-up. *Dorms from 3650 yen • Tel: 0136-44-1171 •* https://www.karimpani-niseko.com

Niseko Backpackers Hostel Tabi-Tsumugi (ニセコ宿たびつむぎバックパッカーズ)
Smaller hostel, which seems better for single travelers. Good location near Kutchan station and a local supermarket, with a kitchen to cook your own food. *Dorms from 3000 yen • Tel: 0136-22-0539 •* https://tabi-tsumugi.net

Owashi Lodge (オオワシロッジ)
Good location in Hirafu town, right next to Niseko Village ski resort. Lots of things to do in the evening, like hang out in the games room, plus vending machines and ski and board hire at discounted rates. *Dorms from 3700 yen • Tel: 0136-55-5111 •* https://owashilodge.com

How to get there and away

By train

From Sapporo, first get to Kutchan station (2 hours, from 1840 yen) and then take a regular bus to Niseko (390 yen to Grand Hirafu or Hirafu Village, 590 yen to Niseko Village, 690 yen to Annupuri). There are some direct services such as the Rapid Niseko Liner, but otherwise a transfer at Otaru is required. Regular trains (not requiring additional seat charges) usually take only 10-15 minutes longer.

By bus

From Sapporo and Chitose Airport, there are many direct bus services in winter (3 hours, from 2600 yen). Outside winter, buses are still available but usually only a few days a week. Check with your chosen ski resort or hostel to see if there are any passes combining a return bus ticket and lift pass, as these are sometimes available for a discounted rate.

By car or motorbike

Niseko is around two hours from Sapporo, one hour from Otaru and two hours from Hakodate. It's best to park at your hotel. *Useful Michi-no-eki roadside stations: Just outside Niseko, on the intersection of Routes 5 and 66 (Mapcode: 398 174 561) • To Hakodate via Route 5 at Mapcodes 730 057 146 and 521 616 330 • To Otaru or Sapporo, halfway up Route 393 (Mapcode 164 161 744)*

Mapcodes - Hirafu: 398 385 630*55, Niseko: 398 202 268*55, Kutchan: 385 811 824*30

Tourist information

Kutchan station has a tourist information center (9am-7pm). There is no official center in Hirafu or around, so ask at your accommodation if you need to book or rent something. Kutchan station has lockers of various sizes.

Noboribetsu Onsen (登別温泉)

Relaxing in the free footbath at Oyunuma in Noboribetsu

One of the best hot spring towns in Hokkaido, if not Japan. Noboribetsu is an excellent choice for budget travelers who want to enjoy a Japanese hot spring, or at least see the interesting volcanic activity that creates such experiences. The town is well set up for tourists, with an excellent choice of free things to do, such as plenty of walking routes and a footbath.

Getting around

The best way to get around Noboribetsu is on foot. The paths between each tourist spot are short, plus it's a great way to escape the tour buses. Maps and signs show where to go, so it's also very easy. Most should be able to do all in a day. It's also possible to drive to some spots.

Things to do

Jigokudani (登別地獄谷)
Also known as Hell Valley, this hellish area has volcanic steam blowing out from under the ground and hot spring water gushing out, then down to the local resorts. The water has reacted with the ground to make a hellish yellow, brown and grey surface, which visitors can safely explore on boardwalks. Very atmospheric and a great place to take some amazing pics. *FREE • 24h • Located a short walk from town*

Tessen-Ike (鉄泉池)
Watch the hot spring water bubbling out of one of its main sources. Bring something to wipe your glasses, this place gets steamy! *FREE • 24h • End of Jigokudani*

Oyunuma Pond (大湯沼)
Sulfurous lake approximately 1 km in circumference. You used to be able to take a boat ride on it, but don't get in, it's 130°c at the bottom! Also next door is Okunoyu (奥の湯), a fascinating bubbling volcanic mud bath. *FREE • 24h • 17-minute walk from Jigokudani, via Oyunuma Nature Trail 1+2, or a short drive from the town • Mapcode: 603 318 005*66*

Oyunumagawa Natural Footbath (大湯沼川天然足湯)

A short walk through this lovely forest leads you to a free hot spring footbath. The water is lukewarm, so will suit anyone. There is also an observatory along the way. *FREE • 24h • Head around Oyunuma Pond, then down the Oyunumagawa Sightseeing Pathway for 10-15 minutes. Walk down road at end to return to town, via the blue Oyaku-kizo statue (親子鬼像) • Mapcode: 603 318 005*66*

Gokuraku Shopping Street (極楽踊り)

Sengen Park and geyser (泉源公園の間欠泉)

You can't miss this noisy hot spring source. It sounds like a monster and kids and adults alike love to see how close they can get. *FREE • 24h • Center of town*

Oni-Bokora statues (鬼祠)

Get yourself a selfie or two in front of these rather gruesome looking monster statues, just opposite Sengen Park. The little shrine next door is also worth a peek if you have time.

Takimotokan (第一滝本館)

While the rooms at this hotel will be out of the price range of many travelers, Takimotokan has some excellent hot spring baths that day visitors can enjoy. Drinking a beer while enjoying a hot spring with a view over Jigokudani really is bliss. This hot spring is regarded as one of the best in Japan, with a huge collection of different baths and great facilities. *9am-4pm: Adults 2000 yen, children 1000 yen. 4pm-6pm: Adults 1500 yen, children 750 yen. Free 24h access if you stay at nearby Takimoto Inn • Across the road from Sengen Park*

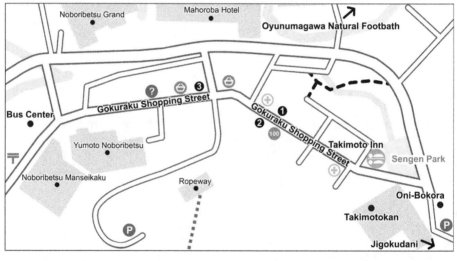

Budget food

Most people staying in one of the expensive hotels here will eat there, so budget travelers should go to one of the convenience stores or check out these places:

1) Isekura (いせくら) - Old-school Japanese BBQ spot, which also has traditional rice bowls and ramen options. *Bowls from 750 yen, small plate dishes from 540 yen • 6pm-1am • Near 7-Eleven*

2) Tenho Ramen (ラーメン天鳳) - Classic, unpretentious ramen bar. *Ramen from 750 yen • 11:30am–2pm, 6–11pm • Opposite Isekura on Gokuraku Shopping Street*

3) Pizzeria Astra - Casual pizza joint. *Pizzas from 500 yen • 11:30am-4pm, 8pm–1am • Between 7-Eleven and Seicomart on Gokuraku Shopping Street*

Cheap supermarkets (スーパー)

While there aren't any big supermarkets in the onsen town, there are a few convenience stores (see map for locations) which sell hot food, as well as sandwiches, cup noodles and microwavable dishes. There is a supermarket on the way from Noboribetsu station called Co-op (コープさっぽろ のぼりべつ東店), which is a five-minute walk north up the main road from the station, that has loads of options to stock up on food (9am-8pm).

100-yen shops

CanDo (キャンドゥ) - Located halfway down Gokuraku Shopping Street. *10am-8pm*

Drugstores (ドラッグストア)

Satudora (サツドラ) has two branches in the town center (10am-10pm).

Recommended cheap accommodation

Takimoto Inn (滝本イン)
Nice budget hotel with reasonably spacious rooms. If you stay here entrance to Takimotokan hot spring is free, just show your room key when entering. Also has a bus service from Sapporo for just 1000 yen. *Rooms from 6630 yen • Tel: 0143-84-2205 •* http://www.takimotoinn.co.jp

Noboribetsu Guest House Aka & Ao (登別ゲストハウス赤と青)
Hostel near the train station, with various types of basic dorm rooms. Sometimes includes free breakfast on Booking.com. *Dorm beds from 2800 yen • Tel: 0143-83-7680 •* https://aka-ao.jp/en/

Nennomori Porotonomori Camping Ground (白老ふるさと２０００年ポロトの森)
Plenty of space for camping, as well as bungalows for reservation, all amongst forest. There are lots of facilities, plus a small shop. Bookings are done over the phone, so ask at a hotel or tourist center before if you want to call. *From 400 yen for adults, 300 yen for children • Tel: 0144-85-2005 • Mapcode: 545 252 612*33 •* http://www.jbbqc.com/poroto_camp/info.html

How to get there and away

By train
There are usually one or two Limited Express trains every hour to Noboribetsu station from Sapporo (75 mins, 3960 yen) or Hakodate (150 mins, 6370 yen). You can also go by local train from Sapporo (2 hours, 2160 yen). Once at Noboribetsu station, take a local bus to Noboribetsu Onsen (340 yen).

By bus
From Sapporo station or the bus terminal there are buses every hour or so to Noboribetsu station (2-3 hours, 1850 yen). From here you can head on the bus to Noboribetsu Onsen (340 yen). Some hotels have direct buses, so be sure to enquire when you book.

By car or motorbike
Noboribetsu Onsen is around three hours from Hakodate, one and a half hours from Sapporo and 50 minutes from Toyako Onsen. *Useful Michi-no-eki roadside stations: To Sapporo via Route 36 at Mapcode 113 413 623 • To Toyako Onsen via Route 453 at Mapcode 321 498 699*

Mapcode: 603 257 766*85 (town center)

Tourist information
The Tourist Information center has lots of extra resources and super helpful staff (9am-5pm).

Toyako Onsen (洞爺湖温泉)

A well built-up tourist town, located on Lake Toya, Toyako Onsen was the site of a huge volcanic eruption in 2000 as well as the location for the G8 Summit in 2008. Due to all this activity, as well as the beautiful lake and hot spring waters, the town has a host of free or cheap things to do and great facilities for all kinds of tourists.

Things to do

Disaster monuments, Konpira craters and Mount Nishiyama walk
See the remains after the volcanic eruptions in 2000, such as torn-away bridges, buried public baths and the odd car in a lake! Very eerie, but fascinating at the same time. Once you have finished the disaster monuments, continue up the path to the newly formed Konpira craters. Continue further for even more deformed roads and abandoned houses towards Mount Nishiyama. *FREE • 1-2 hour walk • Closed at night and in winter • Starts just north of the visitor center*

Sculptures and art around the lake
Head down to the bay, then walk east and west a bit to see some rather striking sculptures and art pieces, such as in the picture above. If you have a car, consider driving around the lake for more, plus the occasional quaint lakeside town to check out. It's also possible to rent bicycles from the tourist center and spend a day biking around the whole lake.

Free foot and hand spas (手湯 + 足湯)
There are several free foot and hand baths around town, including some from which you can enjoy a view over the lake. Pick up a free Toyako Onsen Town Map from the visitor center for locations currently open. Opening times vary.

Nakajima (中島)
Great spot for a bit of light hiking. Nakajima, located in the center of Lake Toya, has hiking routes from just 40 minutes long, to a round course that takes two hours. You'll be taken through lush cedar forests, marshlands and come across the odd forest shrine. *Adults 1420 yen, children 710 yen • 8am-4:30pm (every 30 mins) • Ferry departs from the bay near the visitor center*

Toya Kohantei Hot Spring (洞爺湖畔亭)
If you want more of an authentic hot spring experience and don't mind getting naked, this is the best in town. With an outside bath that looks over the lake, it's an experience that will stay with you for a long time. *Adults 1420 yen, children 710 yen • 2am-10pm • West side of town*

Budget food

It's easy to self-cater, but here are some nice places to try out:

Hydune (ハイドゥン) - Chilled-out burger joint. *Burgers from 600 yen • 11:30am-9pm (Friday to Saturday), 5pm-10pm (Wednesday and Thursday) • Opposite Toyako Manseikaku Hotel*

Wakasaimo (わかさいも) - This gift shop has a restaurant with family favorites such as curry, tempura and sushi. *Meals from 650 yen • 9am-7pm • Down the road past Hotel New Toyako*

Mendokoro (麺処) - Authentic ramen bar. *From 700 yen • 11:30am-3pm • Opposite Wakasaimo*

Cheap supermarkets (スーパー)

It's mostly souvenir shops in the town of Toyako Onsen, but there are also 7-Eleven and Seicomart convenience stores, which have hot food options.

Co-op - Large supermarket a minute down to the right from the station exit (10am-7pm)

Akahane - Small mini-mart near the Toya Green Hotel in town (9am-6pm)

Recommended cheap accommodation

Petit Hotel Koizumi (プチホテル KOIZUMI)

By far the cheapest place we found. You pretty much get your own little apartment for less than a hostel room in a big city. *Beds from 4000 yen • Mapcode: 321 516 049*77*

Guest house HiDE

Very simple rooms with basic facilities like microwaves to cook for yourself, but still much cheaper than some hotels in town. *Beds from 4500 yen • Mapcode: 321 519 464*41*

Green Stay Campsite (グリーンステイ洞爺湖)

A host of rental options, campsites and lodges are available at this serene location on the west side of the lake. *Sites from 4000 yen • Tel: 0142-75-3377• Mapcode: 321 605 817*00*

How to get there and away

By train

Toya station, known as TOYA(JR-MURORAN), is on the line that runs from Hakodate to Sapporo. From Hakodate (2 hours, 4970 yen) or Sapporo (100 mins, 5400 yen), take a Limited Express train to Toya station. From here take a local bus to Toyako Onsen (20 mins, 330 yen).

By bus

From Sapporo station, go to the bus terminal and take a Donan bus to Toyako Onsen (3 hours, 2780 yen, 4-5 per day). Reserve at least a day before at the bus terminal.

By car or motorbike

Toyako Onsen is about 50 minutes from Noboribetsu Onsen, two and a half hours from Hakodate and two hours from Sapporo. There are large parking lots near the visitor center. *Useful Michi-no-eki roadside stations: To Hakodate, 15 minutes out of town via Route 37 at Mapcode 662 267 873 • To Noboribetsu Onsen via Route 453 at Mapcode 321 498 699 • To Sapporo via Route 230, there are some at Mapcodes 321 879 391, 385 256 437 and 759 672 331 to help break up the journey*

Mapcode: 321 518 339*60 (Visitor Center)

Tourist information

Toyako Visitor Center (9am-5pm) is worth heading into to see the exhibitions about the area, as well as a Volcano Museum for a more in-depth experience (adults 600 yen, children 300 yen). Make sure you pick up the free Toyako Onsen Town Map to get around easily on foot.

South Hokkaido

Hakodate (函館)

One of the traditional western-style buildings in Motomachi

One of the first cities in Japan to open up to international trade, Hakodate offers visitors something different from the rest of Hokkaido. Dutch, American, English and other traders came and settled here when Japan opened up more than 150 years ago, creating a rich history and places to visit that feel like a fusion of east and west. Give yourself at least a day to enjoy it all and make sure you try the succulent seafood rice bowls at the morning market.

How to get around Hakodate

Hakodate has a simple tram network that will get you to within a short walking distance of the tourist spots. The sights are a bit far away from each other to do the city solely on foot. Using one of the passes below is highly recommended to save on money and cut out any hassle as you'll need to use public transportation a lot to pack in as many spots as you can.

Discount passes and tickets

Tram One-Day Pass

Allows unlimited use of the trams in Hakodate for one day. As the city is best traveled via tram, this is a must purchase that can take you to all the tourist spots. You'll easily save money as single tickets start at 210 yen. It also comes with a handy city map showing visitors exactly where to stop off for each tourist attraction. Buy at the Hakodate station tourist information center or at some hotels. *Adults 600 yen, children 300 yen.*

Hakodate Bus One-Day Pass (Kanpass)

If you want to be dropped off right outside every tourist spot rather than walk from the nearest tram stop, then this pass would suit you. It allows unlimited use of city buses for one day, including to Goryokaku, Motomachi, the bay area and up Mount Hakodate. There is also a combined ticket that includes the tram too. Buy at the Hakodate station tourist information center. *Kanpass: Adults 800 yen, children 400 yen. Bus + tram combined pass: One day 1000 yen, two days 1700 yen (children half price)*

Things to do

Preparing fresh crab for a morning meal at the Hakodate Morning Market

Hakodate Morning Market (函館朝市)

Known in Japanese as Hakodate Asaichi (literally morning market), this has to be the best fish market in Hokkaido, and one of the most interesting in Japan. An enormous array of all kinds of fish are on offer from more than 250 stalls and restaurants. Make sure you get here early in the day. *FREE • 6am-2pm (January to April), 5am-2pm (May to December) • Just outside Hakodate station*

Bay area (ベイエリア)

A relaxing spot to come for a stroll any time of the day, but especially atmospheric in the early evening. The bay is lined with the historic Kanemori Red Brick buildings, which more than 100 years ago were used as warehouses, but have now been refurbished as shopping complexes with lots of window shopping and some tax-free shopping opportunities at the many boutique shops. *FREE • 24h • Short walk from Jujigai tram stop • Mapcode: 86 041 583*41*

Mount Hakodate (函館山)

This 334-meter high mountain provides an amazing view at night, and while it's a little pricey going up this mountain, it's not to be missed. The view from the top is considered to be one of the three top night views in Japan. A cable car takes visitors to the top, while the observation desks are free. *Ropeway (round trip): Adults 1280 yen, children 640 yen • 10am-10pm (25/4 to 15/10), 10am-9pm (16/10 to 24/4) • By tram: Ropeway is a 10 minute walk from Jujigai or Horaicho tram stops. By bus: There are direct summit buses from Hakodate station for 400 yen (does not operate in winter). By car: Parking spaces are very limited at the top, but there is a road up • Mapcode: 86 009 717*30*

Motomachi (元町)

Hakodate was one of the first ports to open up to foreign trade in Japan. Many foreigners settled in Motomachi, which has created an impressive collection of western-influenced buildings. Some are lit up in the evening, while from December to February the trees lining the streets are decorated with Christmas lights, so it is worth coming back after everything is closed for the day. Some historical buildings require an entrance fee, but you can save money by buying multi-pass tickets at participating buildings. Below are some highlights. *Take the tram to Suehiro-cho or Jujigai. Most sites are about 10 minutes on foot from these tram stops. All the sights are well signposted from the tram stops*

Old Public Hall of Hakodate Ward (旧函館区公会堂)

Designated as an important cultural property, this building has a grand hall and very posh rooms that were used for special guests, such as royal families. Even if you don't go inside, it's worth taking a picture of this magnificent building from the outside. *Adults 300 yen, children 150 yen • Up Moto-saka Dori from Suehirocho tram stop • 9am-7pm (until 5pm November to March). Note that major renovation works are scheduled until 2021 • Tel: 0138-22-1001 • Mapcode: 86 040 434*41*

Hakodate Orthodox Church (函館ハリストス正教会)

Founded by the Russian Consulate in 1859, it's often considered the most visually stunning building in Motomachi. *200 yen donation • Towards the ropeway from the Old Public Hall • Weekdays: 10am-5pm, Saturdays: 10am-4pm, Sundays: 1pm-4pm (closed December 26 to mid-March)*

Old British Consulate (旧イギリス領事館)

Used as the British Consulate from 1913 to 1934, this complex is known for its classical tea room where guests can enjoy a good old cup of British tea while looking over the rose garden. The exhibitions inside are also a great way to learn about the opening of the port and how Hakodate was radically changed due to all the new trade, culture and skills brought over. *Adults 300 yen, children 150 yen • Across from Old Public Hall • 9am-7pm (until 5pm November to March)*

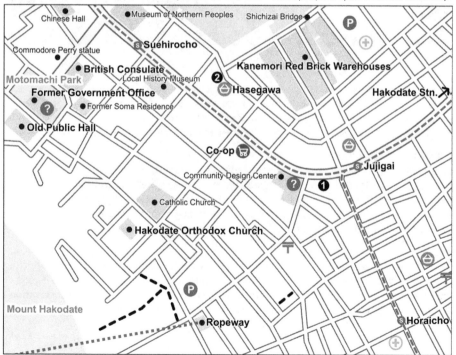

Goryokaku (五稜郭)

Very impressive fort, the first one to be built in Japan based on western designs and structures. There is also the Hakodate Magistrate's Office, which has good English explanations about the fort's long, violent history. Nearby is the tower, which provides splendid views of all the cherry blossoms during that time of the year. *FREE entry to park. Goryokaku Tower: Adults 900 yen, children 450-680 yen, under 5s FREE • 10 minute walk from Goryokaku-koen-mae tram stop • Park: 9am-6pm (5pm in winter). Tower 9am-7pm (6pm in winter) • Mapcode: 86 165 087*55*

Yunokawa Hot Spring foot bath (湯の川温泉足湯湯巡り舞台)

Worth visiting at the end of the day, especially if you have a tram pass, Yunokawa Onsen is towards the end of the line. There is a free foot bath near the tram stop that you can soothe your feet in after all the walking you have hopefully done to save money! *FREE • 24h • Just outside Yunokawa Onsen tram stop • Mapcode: 86 110 366*11*

Hakodate Park (函館公園)

Take some time away from the busy city center and say hello to some local deer at this huge park. It's also a decent place to visit during the cherry blossom season if you happen to be here at that time. *FREE • Short walk from Aoyagicho tram stop • Mapcode: 86 011 281*33*

Volunteer guides and tours

The Hakodate Goodwill Guide Association is an official service that can provide English speaking volunteer guides to take visitors around Hakodate and surrounding areas. Booking before traveling to Hokkaido is advised. Get more information and book at https://hakodategoodwill.wixsite.com/hakodatesgg or email hakodategoodwill@yahoo.co.jp.

Budget food

Most of the national budget restaurant chains don't have stores in central Hakodate, so after the morning market closes definitely consider getting food from a convenience store or cheap supermarket, which are all over the city. Motomachi has some cafes and sweet stores, but they are not really aimed at the budget-conscious travelers looking for a proper meal.

Hakodate Morning Market (函館朝市) - Many of the places in this market will cook or prepare the food in their stall for you, to eat within minutes. It's not just fish here, they have produce from across the prefecture to suit all tastes. Super fresh and super tasty, make sure you don't miss out on this treat! *Fish and rice bowls from around 500-600 yen • 6am-2pm (January to April), 5am-2pm (May to December) • Just outside Hakodate station*

Ajisai Ramen (函館麺厨房あじさい) - Old school ramen joint with an inventive range of toppings. *Ramen bowls from 750 yen • 10am-9:30pm • In Hakodate station and outside Goryokaku Tower*

Mister Donut (ラーメン横丁) - Cheap donuts and light meals. *Donuts from 100 yen • 7am-10pm • Just outside Goryokaku-Koen-Mae tram stop*

Gindaco (築地銀だこ) - Takoyaki (octopus balls). *Light meals from 580 yen • 9am-9pm • Inside the Supaakusu supermarket (スーパーアークス) in the Polestar shopping mall outside Goryokaku station*

Naruto (小樽なると屋) - Traditional Japanese set meals. *From 600 yen • 10am-9pm • In the Polestar shopping mall outside Goryokaku station*

Hasegawa (ハセガワストア) - Convenience stores with a large selection of ready-made meals, such as fried noodles, sushi bowls and yakitori (skewered chicken). *From 600 yen • 24h • 1) West end of bay area, past parking lot. 2) Near Hakodate station, head a few minutes down eastbound tram lines. 3) Near Goryokaku Tower. Head down the road where Ajisai Ramen and Lucky Pierrot are situated, then turn left at second block and walk down a bit.*

Motomachi

1) Sakuraiya (櫻井家) - Welcoming ramen spot with all the classic ingredients. *Ramen bowls from 680 yen • 11am-2pm, 5:30pm-8pm (closed Mondays) • Near Jujigai tram stop*

2) Lucky Pierrot (ラッキーピエロ) - Famous Hakodate burger chain. *Burgers from 350 yen • 10am-9pm • Near to Hasegawa in the bay area. Also one outside Goryokaku Tower*

Cheap supermarkets (スーパー)

Co-op has stores near Jujigai tram stop, towards Suehirocho (9am-9:45pm) and just outside Hakodate Arena-Mae (9am-9pm). Budget supermarket chain MaxValu (マックスバリュ) has stores near the Hakodate Dock-Mae (7am-10pm) and Showabashi (7am-11pm) tram stops.

Shopping

Kanemori Red Brick Warehouses (金森赤レンガ倉庫) - There are countless stores here offering tax-free shopping. Shops specializing in local foods, Japanese toys, trendy souvenirs and cheap cosmetics are scattered around the warehouses. *Various times, but usually 9am-5pm • Near Jujigai tram stop*

Marui (丸井今井店) - Large department store with tax-free store-wide, specializing in fashion and luxury food items. Pastry Snaffles in particular is recommended for those with sweet tastes. *10am-7pm • Outside Goryokaku-Koen-Mae tram stop*

T.O. Department Store (テーオーデパート) - Slightly more down-market than Marui, you'll definitely find some tax-free bargains here. *10am-9pm • A ten minute walk west from Goryokaku-Koen-Mae tram stop along the main road*

100-yen shops

Daiso (ダイソー) - In the Pole Star shopping mall, on the west side of Goryokaku station and inside the T.O. Department Store (函館テーオー店). *10am-8pm*

Drugstores (ドラッグストア)

Daikoku has a store in the morning market (6am-3pm). Sapporo Drugstore has a larger store around the back (7am-5pm), with smaller branches scattered around the tourist areas. Tsuruhadoraggu has a huge store near Omachi tram stop in Motomachi (9am-10pm).

Recommended cheap accommodation

Hakodateyama Guest House (函館山ゲストハウス)

Great, friendly service and reasonably priced Japanese rooms. They also have loads of food and drinks to buy, all for 100 yen each. *Dorm beds from 3000 yen, private rooms from 4500 yen (open April to October) • Ten minutes on foot from Yachigashira tram stop • https://hakog-e.cloud-line.com/ • Mapcode: 951 296 432*41*

Eye Cafe (アイ・カフェ)

Internet café and entertainment complex with large selection of comics and cheap food (showers 350 yen extra). *6 hours (6 時間ナイトパック) from 1250 yen, 9 hours (9 時間ナイトパック) from 1650 yen (100 extra at weekends) • Across the road from T.O. Department Store (函館テーオー店), which is a 10 minute walk west from Goryokaku-Koen-Mae tram stop along the main road • Tel: 0138-55-7771*

Capsule Hotel Hakodate (カプセルホテル函館)

Sleep in small capsules and save on expensive hotel fees. Reasonably modern, with cheap drinks and snacks available, plus free bicycle rental and car parking spots for 500 yen. *Capsules from 3000 yen • Outside Shinkawacho tram stop • https://capsule-hakodate.jp/ • Tel: 0138-24-5001*

How to get there and away

The super fast new Hayabusa Shinkansen trains bring tourists to Hokkaido all the way from Tokyo

By air

Just like Sapporo, it will probably be cheaper to fly if departing from outside Hokkaido, unless you're using a rail pass. Internal Hokkaido flights can be pricey or inconvenient from Hakodate if you don't use one of the discounts on offer from ANA or Japan Airlines.

By train

From Onumakoen station (Onuma Park), take a Limited Express train to Hakodate (25 mins, 1160 yen) or a local train, transferring at Onuma station, to Hakodate (1 hour, 540 yen). From Sapporo take a Limited Express train (4 hours, 5720 yen). If traveling from the south via the Shinkansen, first make your way to Shin-Hakodate-Hokuto station. From here take a Hakodate Liner or other Hakodate bound train to Hakodate station (20 mins, 360 yen).

By bus

From Sapporo station, take a bus directly to Hakodate (5 hours, 4810 yen). Buses leave every two hours or so, including an overnight service if you want to save on accommodation for the night. Book at the bus terminal at least a day before departure.

Mapcode: 86 072 498*85 (Hakodate station)

Tourist information

There are tourist information centers in Hakodate station (9am-7pm in summer, 9am-5pm in winter), at the airport (open till last flight), the Hakodate Community Design Center near the Jujigai tram stop (9am-9pm) and in Motomachi (9am-7pm in summer, 9am-5pm in winter). Hakodate Asaichi also has a booth that can help with tax-free shopping and overseas shipping (8:30am-1pm). If transferring at Shin-Hakodate-Hokuto, there is also one there (9am-7pm).

Onuma Park (大沼公園)

Onuma Park is a national park near to Hakodate, famous for its magnificent lakes and the surrounding forested mountains. It's a worthwhile stop-off on your journey when in south Hokkaido, with some excellent, gentle walks offering splendid views of this tranquil park.

Things to do

There are a variety of walking courses that start nearby to the train station. See the map just outside the station for directions to each course.

Shimameguri-no-Michi walk (島巡りの路)

Known as the island hopping trail, this is the longest walking course, taking walkers to seven islands via some rather lovely old arched bridges. While it is the most popular route, you'll still have moments alone to enjoy the view in peace. The route is well signposted. *Difficulty: Easy • Time required: around 50 minutes*

Mori-no-Komichi walk (森の小径)

Starting at the same point as the Shimameguri-no-Michi walk, this route essentially cuts the course in half. It's therefore a good choice if you feel 50 minutes will be too long a walk. *Difficulty: Easy • Time required: around 20 minutes*

Oshima-no-Michi walk (大島の路)

You could add this walk if you have time. Providing the best views of the grand Mount Komagatake, this paved path course is also known for cherry blossom trees, roses in summer and golden leaves during autumn/fall. This route is probably the easiest and is also fine for baby strollers and those in wheelchairs. *Difficulty: Very easy • Time required: around 15 minutes*

Yuhi-no-Michi walk (夕日の道)

Pretty much devoid of people apart from a few fishermen when we went, this walk seems to be off many tourist maps. It's a peaceful, slightly more rugged walk around the smaller Lake Konuma, which has arguably more interesting wild birds and waterfowl to see than the other busier walks. *Difficulty: Easy • Time required: around 25 minutes*

Onuma Yusen boat trip (大沼合同遊船)

Visitors can also take a tour of Lake Onuma and Lake Konuma via these sightseeing cruises. Taking around 30 minutes, the cruises will give you an even better view of Mount Komagatake, but they are not an essential activity if you have already done the walks. A great option for large families. *Adults 1100 yen, children 550 yen • About every hour from 8:20am-6:20pm, with an extra cruise at 5pm in July and August (operating mid-April to December) • Onuma Park Plaza, which is 10 minutes on foot from the station*

Bike rental

You can also bicycle around Lake Onuma, as well as some of the walking routes. Some of the way around the lake is on roads, but it will get you away from any crowds if you are unlucky enough to be here when a tour bus stops drops by with loads of people! It takes about two hours to go around on a bicycle. Head to Friendly Bear (フレンドリーベア) to rent a bike. They have various types for all ages. *From 1000 yen a day • 9am-5pm • Just outside the station*

Budget food

While there are no good convenience stores or supermarkets nearby, you'll walk by the odd ice cream or yakisoba (fried noodles) stand on your way from the station to the park. Expect to pay 300-400 yen for ice creams and from around 600 yen for a noodle takeaway. Other than these places, there are some strictly average family restaurants, but with Hakodate so close, it's best to avoid them if you can. Here are the best takeaway places if you need a quick meal or snack:

Woods (ウッズ) - Ice cream with funny flavors like wine and squid ink, plus Japanese classics like takoyaki (octopus balls) or yakisoba for takeout. *Takeout meals from 400 yen, ice cream from 300 yen, snacks from 250 yen • 8:30am-4pm • Between station and park*

Fast Foods 56's Goro's (ファーストフーズ 56's) - Soba, udon, takoyaki, butter potato and curry rice; all the Japanese fast food classics. *Snacks from 220 yen, takeout meals from around 400 yen • 9am-4pm • Next to Woods*

Friendly Bear (フレンドリーベア) - Has a stall outside selling cheap snacks, plus a more standard Japanese restaurant inside. *Snacks from 300 yen • 9am-5pm • Just outside the station*

How to get there and away

By train

To reach the park, make your way to Onumakoen station, where most Limited Express trains between Hakodate and Sapporo stop off. From Hakodate station, get a local (38 mins, 540 yen) or Limited Express train (34 mins, 1160 yen). These trains can also pick you up if arriving on the Shinkansen at Shin-Hakodate Hokuto station.

By car or motorbike

Onuma is just 40 minutes from Hakodate, or about two hours from Toyako Onsen. There is a big parking lot near where the walks start. *Useful Michi-no-eki roadside stations: Heading north, there is one a few minutes past the Toyota dealership at Mapcode 490 638 470 (tel. 01374-2-4886)*

Mapcode: 86 815 356*52 (Visitor Center)

Tourist information

There is a big new tourist information center just to the right after exiting the station (8:30am-5:30pm). It has luggage facilities, locally produced snacks and a 'kids corner' for those traveling with little ones. They can also help you to book campsites or other accommodations nearby.

Matsumae Castle (松前城)

Matsumae Castle is the only Japanese-style castle in Hokkaido, being at the northern border of Japan during the Edo Period. It's a worthwhile day trip from Hakodate if you have never been to one or don't plan to visit one elsewhere in Japan. Inside there is an exhibition showing off local historical pieces, but the castle itself is rather small. The grounds are spectacular during the cherry blossom season, with thousands of sakura trees scattered around the town. *Adults 360 yen, children 240 yen • 9am-5pm (closed December 11th to April 9th)*

Getting around

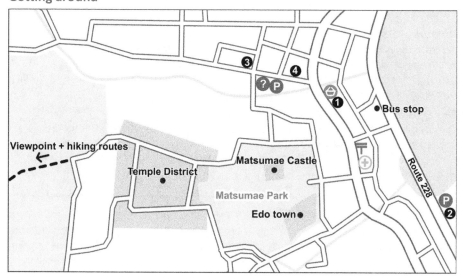

From the bus stop, make your way up to the castle, passing some classy Japanese homes and checking out the main shopping area. Once you are at the castle, it's pretty easy to get around. To the western side of the park there is a small re-creation of the town during the Edo Period, containing about a dozen very authentic and traditional buildings.

To the northwest of the castle grounds is the temple area, full of various free spots to explore. As they are some of the oldest buildings in Hokkaido they are a must see for any visitor. Definitely feel free to explore the other samurai-style neighborhoods or streets lined with cherry blossom trees if they look of interest.

If you are up for a longer walk, then head to the northeast end of the park. Walking up the cherry blossom tree path will bring visitors to a viewpoint with views over the town. If you want more of a proper hike, you can continue up to the Hachijuhakkasho hiking course. Here there are some pleasant hiking trails, with some taking only 20-30 minutes.

Budget food

You'll see some expensive, traditional Japanese restaurants as you approach the castle, but here are some good budget options around the town. See the map for locations.

1) Seicomart (セイコーマート) - Decent convenience store with hot food and microwavable meals. *Takeout meals 350-600 yen • 6am-12am*

2) Kitamaebune-Matsumae (道の駅 北前船松前) - This Michi-no-eki roadside station has a lovely Japanese restaurant overlooking the sea. *Meals from 550 yen • 9am-6pm (5pm in winter)*

3) Shato Pizza House (シャトーピザハウス) - Pizzas, curries, sandwiches and other family favorites. *Meals from 700 yen • 11:30am-10pm (closed Mondays)*

4) Miku Honkan (三久本店) - Wide selection of ramen bowls, as well as some other classic Japanese meals. *Meals from 750 yen • 11:30am-7pm (closed Wednesdays)*

How to get there and away

By train

A good option if you have a rail pass is to take the Hakodate Liner train from Hakodate to Shin-Hakodate Hokuto, then the Shinkansen to Kikonai (40 mins). If you don't have a rail pass and would prefer to do half the trip on the train, then take the South Hokkaido Railway from Hakodate to Kikonai (1 hour, 1110 yen). From Kikonai you then need to take a bus to Matsushiro (90 mins, 1370 yen), of which there are up to ten per day, so you shouldn't need to wait too long. If in Hakodate, buy tickets the day before at the Hakodate Bus Ekimae information desk outside the station.

By bus

There are three buses a day direct from Hakodate (3 hours, 2150 yen). Reserve at least a day before at the Hakodate Bus Ekimae information desk outside the station and make sure you get off at Matsushiro (松代), the nearest stop to the castle.

By car or motorbike

It takes about two hours to drive here from Hakodate. *Useful Michi-no-eki roadside stations: Just outside Kikonai station, at the halfway point from Hakodate, at Mapcode 584 652 022, telephone no. 01392-2-3161 • Just to the south of the castle, at Mapcode 862 028 757, telephone no. 0139-46-2211*

Mapcode: 862 058 252*74 (Matsumae Castle)

Tourist information

The local tourist information center is just outside the castle (9am-5pm).

Daisetsuzan National Park and central Hokkaido

Asahikawa (旭川)

Asahikawa is a large city in central Hokkaido, a convenient transportation hub to stop off at to get some supplies and enjoy city amenities before heading off into the countryside and mountains. The city also has one of the best zoos in Japan, plus is famous for its ramen, but apart from these activities, you won't need to spend too much time here.

Things to do

Asahiyama Zoo (旭川市旭山動物園)
This reasonably big zoo has all kinds of animals on display. The layout of the cages encourages the animals to jump around and play, making the experience more enjoyable for visitors. There are also many feedings and shows to see throughout the day. *Adults 800 yen, children FREE • Summer: 9:30am-5:15pm. Winter: 10:30am-3:30pm • From Asahikawa station, take the bus (routes 41, 42 or 47) to Asahiyama Zoo (40 mins, 440 yen) • Tel: 0166-36-1104 • Mapcode: 79 358 812*82*

Budget food

Asahikawa Ramen
Asahikawa isn't known for much, but it does get praised for its tasty shoyu (soya-based) ramen. The broth is known for being quite oily, with thin noodles and a range of toppings. You'll see some as you walk around the station, but the easiest place to try it is the Asahikawa Ramen Village (あさひかわラーメン村). With eight of the city's best known ramen restaurants all in one place, you'll definitely find something to suit your tastes. *Bowls from 800 yen • Generally 11am-8pm • Short walk from Minami-Nagayama station • Mapcode: 79 410 454*44*

Aeon Mall

Located next to Asahikawa station, this mall has lots of cheap places to eat. Here are the best:
Hanamaru Udon (はなまるうどん) - Cheap, self-service udon (thick noodles) restaurant where customers can choose from a large variety of toppings. *Bowls from 300 yen • 9am-8:30pm*
Pepper Lunch (ペッパーランチ) - Budget teppanyaki chain. *Meals from 750 yen • 9am-9pm*
Gindaco (築地銀だこ) - Takoyaki (octopus balls). *Light meals from 580 yen • 9am-9pm*
Delifrance (デリフランス) - Reasonably priced bakery. *Breads around 130-250 yen • 8am-9pm*

Cheap supermarkets (スーパー)

Aeon Mall, outside the station, also has a large supermarket (8am-10pm).

100-yen shops

Daiso (ダイソー) - Inside the Aeon mall outside the station. *9am-9pm*
Seria (セリア) - Inside Feeeal Mall, behind the Hotel Route-Inn tower. *10am-7:30pm*

Drugstores (ドラッグストア)

Tsuruha Drug (ツルハドラッグ) is to the right as you leave the station from the north exit (7am-9pm). Sapporo Drug (サツドラ) also has a branch in Feeeal Mall (10am-7:30pm)

Recommended cheap accommodation

Mimatsuso Ryokan (美松荘旅館)

Super cheap place with excellent service (free Japanese confectionery and tea on arrival!) and a good location near Asahikawa station. *Rooms from 4200 yen • Tel: 0166-22-6657*

Hotel Kanda (ホテルカンダ)

Business hotel with all the mod-cons you'll need for a good night. *From 5000 yen • Five blocks down main road from station, then to the left a bit •* http://www.hotelkanda.jp/ *• Tel: 0166-29-0100*

Comic Buster (コミックバスターコンパ 37)

Decent net café with a few sleeping options, plus free drinks and showers. *6 hours (6 時間ナイトパック) from 1240 yen, 9 hours (9 時間ナイトパック) from 1650 yen • Walk six blocks down main road to the north of the station, turn left and it's on the left of the second block down • Tel: 0166-21-3249*

How to get there and away

By train

From Sapporo station, take a Limited Express train to Asahikawa (85 mins, 4290 yen). From Furano (1 hour, 1070 yen) or Biei (33 mins, 540 yen) take a local or special Norokko train.

By bus

There are regular buses between Sapporo station and Asahikawa (2 hours, 2060 yen), which are much cheaper than the Limited Express trains if you don't have a rail pass.

By car or motorbike

Asahikawa is around two hours from Sapporo. There are many parking lots in the city center. *Useful Michi-no-eki roadside stations: Coming up from Sapporo via Route 12, there are a few along the way, at Mapcodes 180 276 269 (tel. 01267-2-5775), 360 047 603 (tel. 0125-65-4601), 179 428 432 (tel. 0125-26-5500) and 179 713 597 (tel. 0164-26-3636).*

Mapcode: 79 343 224*63 (Asahikawa station)

Tourist information

The Asahikawa Tourist Information Center is inside the station complex (8:30am-9pm).

Furano (富良野)

Farm Tomita's lovingly curated flower fields

Furano is the most popular place to come in Japan for flower viewing and is best known for its vast lavender fields. The main flower season is between June and September, when all the summer sights will be open, with lots of opportunities to buy lavender based foods, cosmetics and much more. As all the farms are free to enter, budget travelers are spoilt for choice. To see the lavender it's usually best to come around mid-July to the beginning of August. Furano is also an excellent place for winter sports.

Getting around

If coming in summer to see the flowers and lavender fields, start off at Naka-Furano or Lavender-Farm stations, from where all the sights are within walking distance. Once you are done with the spots around one of those stations, you can either walk to the other (around 20-25 mins) or take the special Norokko tourist train. This nostalgic old beast of a train is a great way to get a view over the fields and mountains of Furano. Three to four operate each day, prices are the same as normal trains and you can use a rail pass. Note this train only operates in summer and other trains do not usually stop at Lavender-Farm station. Check http://www.farm-tomita.co.jp/en/ for this year's days of operation.

Things to do

Near Naka-Furano station

Saika no Sato Lavender Farm (彩香の里)
Big flower park, with a decent shop selling off locally produced melons, Japanese sweet potatoes and noodles. Feels less touristy than the other big farms, with fewer tour buses. *FREE • 8am-5pm • 10-15 minute walk from the station • Tel: 0167-56-7970 • Mapcode: 349 244 508*77*

Choei Lavender Farm & Nakafurano Flower Park (中富良野町営ラベンダー園)

This place is a ski slope in the winter, but in the summer it becomes the town's most popular lavender and flower field. It's definitely recommended to walk up to the top for a spectacular view of Mount Tokachidake. You can also take the ski lift if your legs are aching from all the walking! *FREE • 9am-4:30pm • The field is between Naka-Furano and Lavender-Farm stations, so you could pop in along the way between the two (10-15 mins from each station on foot) • Mapcode: 349 246 814*47 • Tel: 0167-44-2123*

Mount Hokuseiyama and forest park (北星山&北星山森林公園管理棟)

At the top of the Choei Lavender Farm, where the ski lift finishes, is this large forest. It's a really quiet place to take a walk, as it's not featured in most tourist maps. There are some small gardens to explore as well, and the view is even better from the top of the forest.

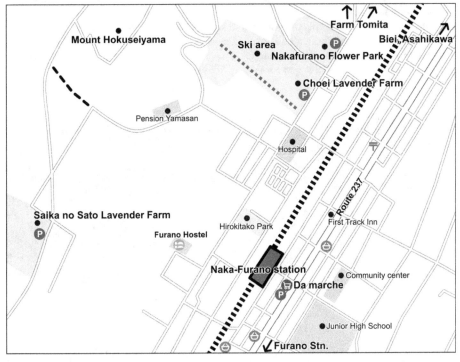

Near Lavender-Farm station

Farm Tomita (ファーム富田)

The most picturesque lavender park in the Furano area, Farm Tomita has a huge variety of flowers and also has a glowing reputation for lavender-themed products, like the delicious lavender ice cream! Because of the site's grand scale you're sure to see something impressive any time during summer. *FREE • 10am-4:30pm • Short, signposted walk from Lavender-Farm station • Tel: 0167 39 3939 • Mapcode: 349 276 804*00*

Lavender East (ラベンダーイースト)

Farm Tomita's sister farm down the road, here the local rice paddies have been converted into lavender fields for production of perfume. It's quieter than Farm Tomita and commands amazing views of the Daisetsuzan mountains to the east. Worth going here if it's on your way via car or if you still have a craving for more lavender fields. *FREE • 9am-4:30pm • By car: short drive from Farm Tomita. On foot: One hour walk from Farm Tomita • Mapcode: 349 251 468*66*

Winter sports and other activities

Apart from the small slope at the Choei Lavender Farm, here are the main activities in winter:

Furano Ski Resort (富良野スキー場)

With great facilities, but quieter than Niseko, Furano Ski Resort is an excellent choice for skiers and snowboarders. With an average of 8 meters snowfall each season, it boasts that it's some of the lightest powder snow in the world. The resort, run by Prince Hotels, opens late November to late March. Note that there is a 'Kids Free Programme' currently on and excellent rental services are on offer.

Full day: Adults 5700 yen, seniors 5100 yen, 12 years and under FREE
Full day early season: Adults 4200 yen, seniors 3700 yen, 12 years and under FREE
Night skiing: Adults 2000 yen, seniors 1800 yen, 12 years and under FREE

Furano Kan Kan Mura

Get into the winter spirit at this snowdome and snow café. The show also has snow sculptures and some nice illuminations, so it's a cool place to chill after or between hitting the slopes. It also has snow tubing for kids and big kids alike! *Adults 300 yen, children FREE • 4pm-9pm (last entry 8pm) • Next to Furano Prince Hotel, near the ski resort ropeway*

Budget food

Tasty lavender and melon ice cream is the perfect way to beat the summer heat

You might want to bring some lunch/dinner with you if visiting the farms or ski resort, as the restaurants can have very touristy prices, and there are not many options around Naka-Furano or Lavender-Farm stations. Just don't forget to try some lavender ice cream (from around 350 yen) or similar tasty treats from one of the farms or lavender fields!

Outside Naka-Furano station there is a Da-marche supermarket (9am-8pm) and there are a few convenience stores on the highway to the east of the station. There are also plenty of convenience stores around Furano station if you are heading there, plus a cheap noodle joint in the station called Keiko Chan no Mise, with prices from 330 yen (9am-6pm). The convenience stores will have basic medicines and a wide selection of meals available.

Recommended cheap accommodation

Furano Hostel (ふらのホステル)
Seems to be the only budget option near to Naka-Furano station. As with most youth hostels, this place won't blow your socks off, but has very cheap dorm beds. Breakfast and dinner are free on some days. *Dorms from 3450 yen •* http://furanohostel.sakura.ne.jp/ *• Tel: 0167-44-4441*

Minshuku Akiba (民宿あきば)
Near Furano station, Minshuku Akiba has some nice Japanese style rooms and some good prices too. Various sizes to suit both independent travelers and families, with shared bathroom facilities. *Rooms from 3600 yen • Tel: 0167-22-3205*

Hoshinitenotodokuoka Camping Ground (星に手のとどく丘キャンプ場)
Situated in quiet surroundings with stunning scenery and plenty of price options for any kind of budget. There are also plenty of facilities, gift shops and a BBQ restaurant. *From 200 yen per site, plus adults 800 yen, children 400 yen • Located 15 minutes by car from Naka-Furano station • Book with Google Translate via* http://www.hoshioka.com/ *or at a tourism information center • Tel: 090-1302-1422 • Mapcode: 349 199 015*00*

How to get there and away

By train
From Sapporo station, you can take a Limited Express train to Asahikawa or Takikawa, then a local train to one of the stations in Furano (2 hours, 3620 yen to Furano station). Check train times at Hyperdia.com. Taking the train is a good choice if you have a rail pass, but otherwise getting the bus from Sapporo is both cheaper and easier. From Asahikawa station, take a local or special Norokko train (1 hour, 1070 yen).

By bus
From Sapporo there are buses all the way to the Furano area every hour (2 and a half hours, 2260 yen, last bus at 6:40pm). There are also buses every hour or two from Asahikawa station to Furano, called the Lavender-Bus (90 mins, 680 yen to Naka-Furano, last bus at 7:40pm). As times are subject to change it's advised to check at the bus offices the day before.

By car or motorbike
Furano is about two hours from Sapporo and one hour from Asahikawa. There are parking lots at most of the farms. *Useful Michi-no-eki roadside station: Towards Asahikawa there is one just outside Biei station at Mapcode 389 011 663, telephone no. 0166-92-0920*

Mapcodes: 349 245 389*77 (Naka-Furano station), 349 276 804*00 (Farm Tomita)

Tourist information

There is a tourist information center in Naka-Furano station (9am-5pm). There is also one next to Furano station (10am-6pm, closed Wednesdays).

Biei (美瑛)

Biei is known all over Japan as one of the best places to go for flower viewing and also for its beautiful countryside hills, almost reminiscent of the Scottish Highlands. The town has become a popular spot for grand walks or bike rides in the countryside. Biei is a pleasant addition to Furano, so give yourself a day to enjoy it all.

Getting around

Unlike Furano, the attractions are quite spread out. If you have a car or motorbike, head straight to each location and use the free nearby parking lots. Here are the options for those without a vehicle:

Rent a bicycle

When the weather is good, this is a delightful way to spend the day. Note that some parts of Biei are a bit hilly, so an electric bike might be worth it. The nearest rental shop to the station is Matsuura, located to the left after exiting Biei station (8am-6pm). There are a few other shops nearby if you want to shop around. Normal bicycles are from 200 yen per hour, electric bicycles from 600 yen per hour.

Walk it!

It may seem a bit nuts, but if you really like a good walk, want to save to the max and think you'll enjoy the countryside more at a slower pace, it's perfectly possible to do it all on foot. Just pick up one of the free walking/cycling maps from the tourist information center. Give yourself a day or long morning to do it all.

Biei View buses

Making scheduled stops at all the highlights around Biei, these buses are a good option for those that just want to relax and enjoy the hotspots. Tours start and end at Biei station, with one course visiting the Patchwork Area and the other visiting the Panorama Area and the Blue Pond. Tours take around two hours. Reservations can be made at least two days in advance at a major JR train station, or you can buy tickets on the day at the tourist information center if there are vacant seats. *Adults 2500 yen, children 1000 yen*

Things to do

Patchwork Area (パッチワークの路)
Situated to the north-west of the station, this area is similar to Naka-Furano, with lavender and flower fields, but spread out among some pristine countryside.

Hokusei-no-oka Observatory (北西の丘)
This park provides tourists with a panoramic view over the Biei countryside from the top of a pyramid-shaped observation desk. The surrounding field also has, as you may guess, lavender. *FREE • 24h • Tel: 0166-92-4445 • Mapcode: 389 070 315*

Zerubu Hill Flower Park (ぜるぶの丘)
Another place to see flowers, Zerubu Hill is full of poppies, lavender and sunflowers in summer. It has some quirky twists, such as multi-colored 'cows' in the fields and mini truck rides around a 'flower course'. *FREE • 8:30am-5pm (April to October) • Tel: 0166-92-3160 • Mapcode: 389 071 595*

Popular trees
There are several trees in Biei that have become famous for being featured in things like TV dramas or commercials. Most popular is the Seven Stars Tree (セブンスターの木), a famous oak tree that was used in old cigarette commercials (Mapcode 389 157 129) and the Ken & Merry Tree (ケンとメリーの木), which was featured in commercials in the 1970s (Mapcode 389 071 727). Neither are essential visits, but worth popping by if on the way somewhere.

Panorama Road Area
Not as easy to access and hillier than the Patchwork Area, the Panorama Area to the south-east of the station has similar sights, but they are far more spread out and much quieter. A good idea is to do the Patchwork Area first, then come here if you feel you need more.

San-ai-no-Oka (三愛の丘展望公園)
Amazing views of the mountains and rolling hills are on offer at this simple park. A good point to head for if on a bicycle. *FREE • 24h • Mapcode: 349 792 477*

Shikisai-no-Oka Flower Park (四季彩の丘)
Actually nearer to Bibaushi station, it's only worth coming here if you have a car. The 15 hectares of land is filled with flowers in bloom from spring to fall, and also has superb views. *FREE • 24h • Tel: 0166-95-2758 • Mapcode: 349 701 160*

Shirogane Blue Pond (青い池)
This beautifully luminescent blue pond is definitely worth checking out if you have a car and are heading to Fukiage Onsen. Made by accident as a result of efforts to control mudslides, aluminum seeped into the water causing it to turn luminescent. *FREE • 24h • On the way to Fukiage Onsen via Route 966 (20 minutes from Biei), or accessible with a Biei View bus tour. Alternatively, you can take a Dohoku Bus bound for Shirogane Hot Spring and stop off at the Blue Pond (25 mins, 540 yen). Enquire at the tourist information office for current pickup point and times (departs from Biei at 6:55am, 9:26am, 12:11pm, 3:46pm and 5:26pm at the time of writing) • Mapcode: 349 568 888*

Budget food

As with Furano, consider bringing food with you or grabbing something from the supermarket or a convenience store. You'll also come across some quaint little cafes and bakeries as you travel around, but here are some takeout and eat-in options that are best for budget travelers:
Koi-ya (戀や) - Classic family-friendly meals, like curry rice, noodles and gratin. *Budget lunch menu 600-1000 yen • 11am to when everything is sold out • Outside Biei station*

Tsuboya (壺屋) - Nice little bakery. *Breads around 150-250 yen each • 9am-7pm • Next to Koi-ya*

Daimaru (だいまる) - More family favorites with a wide selection of meals. *Lunch sets from 880 yen • 11am-3:30pm • Head to the left down the main road from the station (Route 213), Daimaru is just before it meets Route 966 (10 minute walk)*

Hokusei-no-oka Observatory - There are a few stalls selling all kinds of locally produced Japanese takeaway foods and treats, such as sweet potatoes, asparagus and fresh melon pieces. *Snacks and light meals from 300 yen • Around 9am-6pm • Across the road from the observatory*

Cheap supermarkets (スーパー)

There is a big supermarket in the direction of the Patchwork Area. Called Super Chain Fuji (スーパーチェーンふじ), it's located to the north of the station, where Route 966 and the highway meet (8:30am-9pm, 0166-92-3332). Nearer to the station, there is a 7-Eleven (24h) convenience store (just head right from the exit, walk two blocks and you'll see it to your left).

Drugstores (ドラッグストア)

Tsuruha Drug (ツルハドラッグ) is across the road from the supermarket (9am-10pm).

Recommended cheap accommodation

Biei Potato no Oka Youth Hostel (ペンション ポテトヴィレッジ美瑛ポテトの丘)

All sorts of accommodation, from dorm beds to private cottages, are available at this rather plush hostel. Free pickup from Biei station is also on offer with some bookings. *Beds from 3000 yen • Tel: 0166-92-3255 •* https://www.potatovillage.com/

Koeru (こえる)

Located just to the north of the station, this place also has a variety of rooms, but this location can't be beaten. *Rooms from 5593 yen • Tel: 0166-92-5531 •* http://www.biei-koeru.jp/

How to get there and away

By train

There are trains to Biei from Naka-Furano (26 mins, 540 yen) and Furano (36 mins, 640 yen), plus the Norokko tourist train will also stop here in summer from Lavender-Farm station (23 mins, 450 yen). Normal trains operate about once an hour, so check the schedule board at your station to make sure you aren't waiting around too long for the next departure.

By bus

The Lavender-Bus for Furano from Asahikawa will also stop off at Biei station (1 hour, 620 yen). If the timings are good, you might be able to take it from Furano to Biei, but as prices are the same as the train, taking the train is probably easier.

By car or motorbike

Biei is about 40 minutes from Asahikawa, 30 minutes from Furano and two and a half hours from Sapporo. Just like Furano, there are parking lots at most of the farms, or space on the road to park. *Useful Michi-no-eki roadside station: Just outside Biei station at Mapcode 389 011 663, telephone number 0166-92-0920*

Mapcode: 389 010 596*85 (Biei station)

Tourist information

The Tourist Information Center is to the left as you exit Biei station (8:30-5pm). There are also coin lockers at the station if you don't want to take all your luggage around with you.

Asahidake (旭岳)

Mount Asahidake is one of the most famous mountains in Japan, and an excellent place to come in summer or autumn for a hike or two. The village of Asahidake Onsen is a small hot spring town at the bottom of Asahidake mountain, which provides a great place to start or relax at the end of a hike. There are only a dozen or so buildings here, and it does feel a little off the beaten track, but it's still super easy to get to and is quite well set up for tourists.

Things to do

Asahidake Ropeway (大雪山旭岳ロープウェイ)

A handy way to cut out the hardest part of the hike up Mount Asahidake, the ropeway provides an amazing view over the volcanic area. It will also suit those who just want to take pictures and drink a beer while enjoying the splendid view from up top. *Round-trip price (high season/low season): Adults 2900/1900 yen, children 1450/900 yen. One-way price (high season/low season): Adults 1800/1300 yen, children 900/650 yen. High season is June to September • Times vary day by day, so check* http://asahidake.hokkaido.jp/en/ *before visiting • At end of road to Asahidake Onsen • Tel: 0166-68-9111 • Mapcode: 796 861 036*11*

Climb Mount Asahidake (旭岳)

Start early and give yourself the day to see all the fascinating and steamy volcanic activity as you hike up this grand mountain, one of Japan's classic hikes and a rite of passage for all Japanese hikers. Snow can sometime remain on the first part into spring, so ask about routes at the Asahidake Visitor Center before going up. The best time to come for a hike is late June through to September. *Difficulty: Medium • Time required: about 6-8 hours (cut in half if using ropeway) • Route up starts from parking lot outside the ropeway. Well signposted all the way*

Hikes around the village

There are also plenty of lighter hiking and walking trails that start from the village. They are often signposted, but you can also get a free map from the visitor center. Options include a one hour circular course around the ropeway station at the top of the mountain, where walkers will come across sulfurous vents and ponds. There are also many walks back down around the village, which take tourists through the forests surrounding Asahidake.

Hike to Sounkyo Onsen (層雲峡温泉へのハイキング)

Looking to really push yourself and do a multi-day hike? This mega journey across the mountains is for you! The hike takes you through some dramatic volcanic areas and mountains, plus has a free hot spring called Nakadake Onsen (中岳温泉) if you take a little detour. Visitors can stay in a mountain hut for a reasonable fee, plus camping may be OK if the weather is calm. Be sure to head to the Asahidake Visitor Center to check weather conditions, book your night and get a proper hiking map. *Difficulty: Medium • Time required: 1-2 days (cut off a few hours if using ropeways) • Route up starts from parking lot outside the ropeway*

Budget food

Limited food options are available at some hotels, the visitor center and the ropeway stations, so it's highly recommended that you bring food with you from somewhere like Asahikawa, Biei or Furano. If you really need a hot curry or soup, the ropeway has a restaurant with snacks from 300 yen and meals from around 600-800 yen (10am-4:30pm).

Recommended cheap accommodation

If you just want to hike Asahidake, you can do everything in a day trip, but here are some good options if you want to stay the night:

Daisetsuzan Shirakabasou (大雪山白樺荘)

Both western and Japanese rooms are available at this hostel, plus breakfast and dinner options can be added on. Also has a little shop. *Dorm beds from 6530 yen, private rooms from 8940 yen • Mapcode: 796 830 564*47 • Tel: 0166-97-2246 •* http://shirakabasou-asahidake.com/

Asahidake Youth Camp Field (旭岳青少年野営場)

Pleasant campsite with toilet, kitchen and other essentials on site. *Adults 500 yen, children 200 yen • Open mid-June to end of September • 10 minutes from ropeway on foot or a few minutes by car. Take a left after passing Daisetsuzan Shirakabasou • Check availability before at 0166-97-2544 (ask at a visitor center if you don't speak Japanese) • Mapcode: 796 830 292*41*

How to get there and away

By bus

From Asahikawa station, take a bus to Asahidake (90 mins, 1430 yen). At the time of writing, there are buses from Asahikawa station at 7:11am, 9:41am, 1:11pm and 3:41pm, with buses returning at 9:30am, 12pm, 3:30pm and 6pm (check at bus office or a tourism office before). Note there are no direct buses from Biei or Furano, but both the Lavender-Bus (Furano to Biei to Asahikawa) and the Asahidake bus stop at Asahikawa Airport, so you could transfer there. If doing so get the first bus of the day and grab an early lunch at the airport while you wait.

By car or motorbike

Asahidake is about one hour's drive from Asahikawa. There is parking outside the ropeway station. *Useful Michi-no-eki roadside station: There is one about half way from Asahikawa via Route 1160 in a town called Higashikawa at Mapcode 389 406 315, telephone number 0166-68-4777*

Mapcode: 796 861 036*11 (ropeway parking lot)

Tourist information

The visitor center is located a little bit before you get to the ropeway (9am-5pm).

Sounkyo Onsen (層雲峡温泉)

Hiking up Mount Kurodake from Sounkyo Onsen

Sounkyo Onsen is a famous hot spring town in the Daisetsuzan National Park, surrounded by sheer cliffs hundreds of meters high, and mountains hundreds of meters into the sky. Quite well equipped for budget tourists, it's also a great place to start a hike into the unspoiled mountains and forests of Hokkaido. Asahidake offers similar experiences, so if you only have time for one, go for the place that has the best accommodation prices for when you want to visit. Also note Sounkyo Onsen has a free foot bath!

Things to do

Daisetsuzan Sounkyo Kurodake Ropeway (黒岳ロープウェイ)
Get a panoramic view of the Daisetsuzan mountains as you make your way up to 1300 meters, to near the top of Mount Kurodake. From here you can walk to the summit, or take the chairlift half way. *Ropeway round-trip price: Adults 1950 yen, children 1000 yen. One-way price: Adults 1100 yen, children 550 yen. Chairlift round-trip price: Adults 600 yen, children 400 yen. One-way price: Adults 400 yen, children 250 yen • 8am-4pm (closed early January to mid-March) • South end of town • Tel: 01658-5-3031*

Climb Mount Kurodake (黒岳)
A stunning hike up to one of the tallest mountains in this national park. Not crowded at all and lots of amazing views as you climb up above the clouds. *Difficulty: Medium • Time required: 7-8 hours from the bottom or 3-4 hour return walk from ropeway • Entrance to trail is a short walk from the ropeway*

Momojidani Nature Trail (紅葉谷)
A perfect option for those looking for a less taxing walk. The town is one of Hokkaido's top spots for Autumn colors, and this light hiking trail is the most peaceful way to see it. Bring your camera, as you're sure to take some stunning pictures any time of the year. *Difficulty: Easy • Time required: about 1-2 hours • Down the road past Hotel Taisetsu*

Hike to Asahidake (旭岳へのハイキング)

This classic multi-day hike can also be started on this end too. You can stay in a mountain hut along the way (book at a visitor center), which is a great way to cut up the long journey. If you stayed there, then got up early the next day you should be able to reach Asahidake in good time. The hike takes you through some amazing volcanic areas and mountains, and as mentioned is one of the best hikes in Japan. *Difficulty: Medium • Time required: 1-2 days (cut off a few hours if using ropeways) • Entrance to trail is a short walk from ropeway*

Foot bath (足湯)

The town has a lovely little hot spring foot bath to soothe your feet after hiking up Mount Kurodake. *FREE • 24h • Half way up the promenade*

Choyotei Hot Spring (層雲峡 朝陽亭)

This hot spring has an amazing view of the mountains and the best outside baths in town, so it's the perfect spot to come if you are looking for the full hot spring experience in pleasant surroundings. Some baths alternate everyday between male and female use. *800 yen • 1pm-8pm • Up the road from the Taisetsuzan Sounkyo Shrine*

Kurodake No Yu Hot Spring (黒岳の湯)

Certainly not as luxurious as Choyotei Hot Spring, but this very down-to-earth hot spring is the cheapest place to get your full onsen fix. *600 yen • 10am-9pm • Located on the promenade*

Ryusei Falls (流星の滝) and Ginga Falls (銀河の滝)

Two grand waterfalls near the village, with the water dropping from the sheer cliffs hundreds of meters high. These two are said to be the most beautiful in the national park. *FREE • 24h • Five minutes' drive down Route 39, turn right soon after exiting the village and enter the parking lot. If you don't have a car, you could hitchhike or walk down the road (about 40 minutes on foot).*

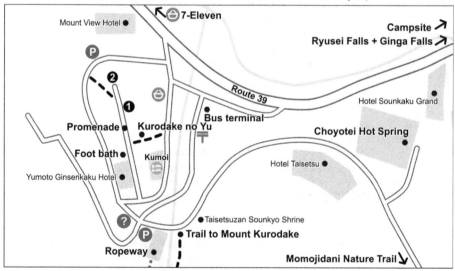

Budget food

While there are no supermarkets or large drugstores for cheap food, there are some convenience stores. Seicomart (7am-11pm) is on the north end of town, while the better 7-Eleven (24h) is a short walk down the highway (Route 39), past the Sounkyo Kankou Hotel. Otherwise check out the following places.

1) Daisetsuzan Shokudo (大雪山食堂) - Many different types of ramen and rice dishes, with budget set menus and gyoza dumplings on offer. *Meals from 700 yen • 10am-9pm • Village center*

2) Ramen House Tozanken (ラーメンハウス登山軒) - Old-school ramen joint. *Ramen from 800 yen • 10am-10pm • North end of the village center*

Simple, hearty food like this is all you'll need after a long hike

Recommended cheap accommodation

Kumoi (ホテル雲井)

Kumoi offers Japanese-style rooms with private or shared bathrooms. There is also a fancy lounge to relax in and play a game of darts or shoot some pool in the evening. *Rooms from 6480 yen • Tel: 0165-853-553 •* https://www.hotelkumoi.com/

Sounkyo Camping Site (キャンプ場)

There is a campsite just to the east of town, as well as one on the way to Asahikawa, so you have various choices of accommodation, from little cottages to tent spaces. Enquire at the visitor center for what's available and exact locations before heading off. *From around 1000 yen*

How to get there and away

By bus

You can access the town via the buses from Asahikawa station (2 hours, 2100 yen) and Kamikawa station (35 mins, 870 yen), which is the nearest the train station. Buses from Kamikawa depart about every hour until 8pm, while Asahikawa has departures at 9:15am, 10:45am, 12:15pm, 2:35pm, 3:45pm, 4:35pm and 6:40pm. As ever, check bus times at least the day before, as they are very much subject to change.

By car or motorbike

Sounkyo Onsen is one hour from Asahikawa and just over two hours from Abashiri. *Useful Michi-no-eki roadside station: At about halfway from Abashiri via Route 39 at Mapcode 402 600 195, telephone number 0157-45-3373*

Mapcode: 623 204 600*00 (visitor center)

Tourist information

The Sounkyo Visitor Center is just across the road from the ropeway station (8am-5:30pm).

Fukiage Onsen (吹上温泉)

The open-air bath at Fukiage Onsen, known in Japanese as a 'rotenburo'

Fukiage Onsen has to be our favorite hot spring in Hokkaido, offering visitors a very authentic bathing experience. Up in the Daisetsuzan mountains to the east of Furano, it's a world away from hot spring villages that can become quite touristy at times, and it's a very easy and cheap to access spot if you do a bit of pre-planning. It's the perfect 'out in the sticks' hot spring experience for budget travelers.

Things to do

Fukiage Hot Spring Outside Bath (吹上温泉露天風呂)
Natural hot spring up the mountain with stunning views down below into the countryside, away from any noise and most tourists. A true hot spring experience, just note that it's mixed and there may be lots of naked people! *FREE • 24h • Outside the 'Fukiage Ikoi no Hiroba' bus stop (show 吹上いこいの広場 to bus driver to be sure you get off at the right stop)*

Hakugin-so and Fukiage Hot Spring Recreation Center (吹上温泉保養センター)
Using the same source as the free outside bath, this center has a wide selection of both inside and outside baths. There are so many types it will take you a while to get them all done, plus there is a mixed swimsuit area for families which has fun slides and much more. A great place to relax after or before some hiking. *Adults 600 yen, children 200-400 yen (FREE if staying at the lodge) • 9am-10pm • Next to Hakugin-so bus stop*

Hiking in Daisetsuzan National Park
Get yourself a hiking map at Hakugin-so before heading up, and check current conditions with them as these can significantly affect which routes you can take. There are also some free mountain huts (山小屋) in the mountain ranges that you can stay at, so ask about these as well if you're interested.

Hike up Mount Sandanyama (三段山)

The surrounding area is full of forests and interesting volcanic landscapes. There is a wide selection of routes, but the most spectacular and easiest is to hike up Mount Sandanyama. It'll probably get rather windy up the top, but hiking above the clouds and looking down over the countryside feels like quite an achievement. Note that the route to Tokachidake Onsen via Mount Sandanyama was blocked at the time of writing. *Difficulty: Medium • Time required: 3-4 hours return journey to the summit of Mount Sandanyama • Trail starts near the Hakugin-so lodge*

Hike up Mount Tokachidake (十勝岳)

Choose this if you're looking for a longer, more energizing hike, this popular day long hike takes visitors up to the summit (2077 meters high). The views, especially during the autumn colors, are pretty mind-blowing when you finally reach the top. Once you are at the summit, you can continue down to Tokachidake Onsen, another hot spring spot which has bus connections back to Fukiage. *Difficulty: Medium • Time required: 6-8 hours return journey to the summit of Mount Tokachidake • Trail starts near the Hakugin-so lodge*

Budget food

It's a good idea to bring some food to cook in the kitchen at Hakugin-so or outside if camping. There is a little shop in the lodge, which has some life-savers such as instant noodles.

Recommended cheap accommodation

Hakugin-so (白銀荘)

This place blew us away with its friendly atmosphere, low prices and stunning views. The dorm rooms are compact, yet very quiet and comfortable. There are also private Japanese rooms and camping spots available, plus hot spring access at the recreation center is included with the lodging fee. *Beds from 2600 yen (last admission 9pm) • Tel: 0167-45-4126 • Mapcode 796 032 434 •* http://kamifurano-hokkaido.com/

How to get there and away

By bus

There are only three buses a day, so be careful you don't miss them and double check the times at a tourism center before you go. Buses depart from Kami-Furano (a short train ride from Naka-Furano) at 8:52am, 12:49pm and 4:31pm, returning from Hakugin-so at 10:01am, 1:51pm and 5:40pm (30 mins, 500 yen). If hiking up Tokachidake and down to Tokachidake Onsen, you can get on the bus there (which is the end of the line) and return to Fukiage Spa (10 mins, 200 yen) or Kami-Furano (40 mins, 500 yen) at 9:45am, 1:37pm or 5:27pm.

By car or motorbike

It takes about 30 minutes to drive here from Biei or Furano. There is plenty of free parking outside the Hakugin-so lodge and a bit near the open-air hot spring.

Mapcode: 796 032 434 (Hakugin-so lodge), 796 031 238*22 (open-air hot spring)

Tourist information

There is no tourism information center, but the Hakugin-so lodge is always happy to give out advice, and have additional free maps and materials for the area.

Akan Mashu National Park and south-east Hokkaido

Kushiro Marshlands (釧路湿原)

Kushiro Marshlands is Japan's biggest marshland and a hotspot for wildlife. The area is a haven for red-crowned crane, known in Japan as 'tancho', as well as a variety of plant life. The crane are known to dance and play together, to the awe of the adoring crowds taking their videos and pictures. The vast scenery stretches nearly 200 square kilometers, with miles and miles of meandering rivers and lush wetlands. The marshlands are located near the city of Kushiro, a convenient place from where to start your trip.

Things to do

Kushiro Shitsugen Norokko train (くしろ湿原ノロッコ号)

Taking this special tourist train is a no-brainer if you have a rail pass. Picking up tourists from Kushiro station, it takes you to the special station at Kushiro Shitsugen (Kushiro Marshlands) and Toro (convenient if you are staying at the hostel or campsite there). Along the way on this wonderfully quaint old train the on-board guide will point out any wildlife outside, such as cranes or deer. From Kushiro Shitsugen station, make your way up to the Hosooka viewpoint (15 minutes on foot) for a panoramic view across the marshlands. *FREE with a rail pass or 360 yen • From Kushiro station at 11:06am and 1:35pm (operates July to late September, with limited service to early October) • Times subject to change, so confirm and reserve your seat at Kushiro station beforehand*

Tancho Observation Center & Akan International Crane Center (ツルセンター)

It's possible to visit the above Hosooka viewpoint by car as there is plenty of free parking near the visitor lounge there (Mapcode 149 654 674*06, telephone number 0154-40-4455). On the other hand, if you really want to see the famous cranes, then seriously consider the Tancho Observation Center. It is one of the feeding stations for local cranes during the cold winter months, and visitors will have a pretty good chance to observe the cranes, especially during feeding times (you can check today's times at the tourist information desk in Kushiro station). The Akan International Crane Center is a breeding sanctuary, where you can see crane any time of the year. There are English explanations about the ecology of the marshlands, as well as the crane and other wildlife. *470 yen for both • Tancho Observation Center: 8:30am-4pm (until 4:30pm February and March, closed April to October). Akan International Crane Center: 9am-5pm (all year) • There are four or five buses a day from Kushiro station (1 hour, 1450 yen), which also continue onto Lake Akan. Get tickets at the bus terminal outside the Kushiro station • Tel: 0154-66-4011 • Mapcode: 556 183 883*85*

Budget food

Eating options are slim at the marshlands, so it's highly recommended to eat in Kushiro or at least pick up some food to eat later. The large supermarket here might also be worth going to if heading north, such as to Lake Mashu, where large supermarkets are scarcer.

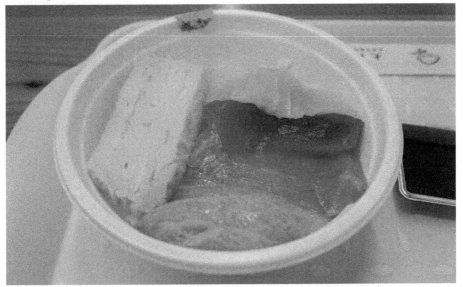

An example of the simple, yet succulent, rice bowls from the Washo Market

Kushiro Washo Market (釧路和商市場) - In Kushiro city this is the only place you should be eating lunch at. It is full of super fresh sushi and sashimi right from the fishing line, and you can customize your rice bowl to contain just the fish you want to eat. *Meals 500-1000 yen • 8am-5pm (closed Sundays) • From Kushiro station, south exit, head to the right down the main road. The market is at the second block, opposite the parking lot*

L'airbon (レフボン) - Simple bakery that can also make dirt cheap sandwiches for you from the window. *Sandwiches from 125 yen • 7am-7:30pm • Inside Kushiro station*

Onigiri BanBan (おにぎりや ばんばん) - Little kiosk selling handmade rice snacks and cheap takeouts. They also have a soba restaurant next door if you would prefer to eat in. *Snacks from 50 yen, meals from 390 yen • 8am-6pm • Inside Kushiro station*

Cheap supermarkets (スーパー)

The Big Kawakita (ザ・ビッグ川北店) is a large supermarket 10 minutes on foot from Kushiro station (8am-9pm). From the south exit, head left and proceed down the road until you get to a bridge over the rail track. Head over the bridge and you'll see the supermarket on the right.

100-yen shops

Daiso (ダイソー) - Next to the Big Kawakita supermarket. *10am-8pm*

Drugstores (ドラッグストア)

Tsuruha Drug (ツルハドラッグ) is also next to the Big Kawakita supermarket (9am-10pm).

Recommended cheap accommodation

Kushiro Shitsugen Youth Hostel (釧路湿原とうろユースホステル)

Surrounded by the wildlife and nature of the Kushiro Marshlands, this is a very relaxing spot to stay the night. You can either stay in shared dorms or book out a group room. *Beds from 3972 yen • Tel: 015-487-2510 • Located just outside Toro station •* http://www.tohro.net/

Guest House Proof Point (ゲストハウス プルーフポイント)

Modern guest house in Kushiro city with well-maintained dorms, free wifi and a comfy lounge area. *Dorm beds from 3660 yen • 5 minute drive or bus ride from Kushiro station • Tel: 0154-65-5527*

Toro Campsite (塘路元村キャンプ場)

A short walk or drive from Toro station, this campsite has basic facilities and a lovely position near the river. *FREE • Open March to October • Tel: 015-487-2172 • Mapcode: 576 841 050*03*

How to get there and away

By air

Budget airline Peach flies here from Osaka. Japan Airlines, Air Do and ANA have flights from Tokyo, while ANA has flights from New Chitose Airport and Japan Airlines has flights from Sapporo Okadama Airport. Additionally, there are some flights from Taiwan, Hong Kong and South Korea. There is a bus service after each flight that takes passengers to Kushiro station.

By train

From Sapporo, take a Limited Express train to Kushiro (4 and a half hours, 6260 yen). From Mashu station in the north, take a train on the Senmo line (80 mins, 1640 yen). There are coin lockers in the station if you want to leave your luggage while you visit the marshlands.

By bus

There are five highway buses every day to/from Sapporo (6 hours, 5770 yen), including a night bus if you want to save on accommodation costs and don't want to waste such a long time on the bus. In Kushiro, you can buy tickets at the bus terminal just outside Kushiro station. You can also buy tickets and check times at Japan Bus Online.

By car or motorbike

Kushiro is just over an hour from Mashu and four hours from Sapporo (break up the journey by dropping into Obihiro on the way). There is a parking lot on the north side of the station.

Mapcode: 149 256 488*74 (Kushiro station)

Tourist information

The helpful tourist information desk is located inside Kushiro station (9am-5:30pm).

Lake Mashu (摩周湖)

Known as the 'mountain god's lake', Lake Mashu is a huge caldera lake in the Akan Mashu National Park. Said to be the second clearest lake in the world, it has a grand perimeter of almost 20 kilometers and has a water level that mysteriously never changes, even after heavy rain. The area can get foggy at times, so it can be a bit hit and miss going there, but it's still an excellent choice for budget travelers looking for a different experience in the mountains.

Discount pass: Teshikaga Eco Passport

This pass is worth getting if you end up needing to take more than two buses every day while in Lake Mashu and Kawayu Onsen. Allowing unlimited use of the buses in the area for a set number of days, it's available to buy on the buses and at tourist information centers such as in Mashu station. *2 days: Adults 1500 yen, children 500 yen. 3 days: Adults 2000 yen, children 700 yen*

Things to do

Lake Mashu via the First Observatory (摩周第一展望台)
Various viewing decks with amazing views over Lake Mashu and the beautiful mountains around its rim. There is also a large shop with plenty of cool local foods and products to buy tax-free. Particularly famous is the locally produced melon, which you can just get a slice of to keep costs down. *FREE (parking 410 yen) • 24h • There are just two buses a day from Mashu station (operates early February to mid-March and from April to mid-July only), departing at 10:30am and 1:15pm, then returning at 11:25am and 2:10pm (25 mins, 560 yen). Buses from Kawayu Onsen (mid-July to early October 8) depart at 8:35am, 10:45am and 1:35pm, then return at 9:25am, 11:45am and 2:20pm (25 mins, 560 yen) • Tel: 015-482-2200 • Mapcode 613 781 339*63*

Hiking to the observatory (美留和〜摩周展望台登山道)
As you can see from the bus times above, public transportation is limited. Thankfully the kind fellows at Tabibitoyado Shoei pointed out this hiking route to us. Instead of taking the bus there, it's possible to hike all the way to the observatory from Biruwa station, giving you more flexibility to do things at Lake Mashu. Actually part of a 71km walk called 'The Ranch Way', this 6.2km section takes walkers through an old farm, then via a dense white birch tree forest up

to the observatory. Recommended is to get the first train from Mashu, at 7:28, then return on the last bus at 2:10pm, giving you plenty of time to hike and enjoy the observatory. *Difficulty: Medium • Time required: around 3 hours • From Mashu station, make your way to Biruwa station (9 mins, 230 yen). Right outside the station you'll see a map and hiking post with 'RANCHWAY' written on it (these are the signs you need to follow). Proceed down the road, and follow the red signs, posts, tape and flags with 'RANCHWAY' or 'KIRAWAY' written on them. Please note that, while the route is signposted, the signs are not well maintained and some are missing. If you don't see any for 10-15 minutes, head back to the last sign to check you didn't make a wrong turn.*

Hiking up Mount Mashu (摩周岳)

This trail takes hikers on a route around the lake and up to the top of Mount Mashu at a height of 857 meters, giving spectacular views to those that complete the challenge. If you don't have a vehicle, consider hitchhiking back into town after doing this hike as the buses will probably leave too early. *Difficulty: Medium • Time required: 5-6 hours return • Starts from the car park*

Lake Mashu Third Observatory (摩周第三展望台)

Worth a visit if you have your own vehicle, this observation area lies a little further north along the western side of Lake Mashu. Consisting of two observation decks providing unobstructed views over the lake, it's quieter than the first observatory. Free parking available. Note that the second observatory is currently closed to the public. *FREE • 24h • Up Route 52 from the first observatory. There is no public transportation here • Mapcode: 613 870 628*28*

Popo foot bath (ぽっぽ湯)

Super-hot foot bath conveniently placed outside the station. Head here after your hike, just don't get too relaxed and miss your train! Free cushions are available from the tourist desk inside the station. *FREE • 24h • Just to the left from the exit of Mashu station*

Budget food

The Mashu-don at Poppotei. We went for 'Special size'!

While there is no sprawling town center with lots of restaurants to choose from, there are luckily some good options at key locations on your travels.

Poppotei - Cozy place to try the local specialty, Mashu Butadon, pork loins on rice with a special BBQ sauce. Other classics, like ramen and curry rice are also on the menu. *Bowls from 620 yen • 10am-7pm • Outside Mashu station, to the left*

Mashu Station - The station has a little shop where you can buy Mashu Butadon bento boxes and more. *Bento boxes 800-1000 yen • 9am-5pm*

Lake Mashu First Observatory - Simple meals like ramen and curry. *500-800 yen • 8am-5pm*

Michi-no-eki Mashu Onsen - Pop into this roadside station if you have your own transport. Offers traditional Japanese meals and also has another free foot bath! *Meals 600-1000 yen • 8am-6pm • Mapcode 462 849 665 • Tel: 015-482-2500*

Cheap supermarkets (スーパー)

There is a Co-op supermarket just across the river from Mashu station, behind the large car park (9am-6pm). If driving, there is a larger supermarket called Fukuharamashuten (フクハラ 摩周店) where Routes 243 and 241 intersect (10am-9pm, phone number 015-482-2318).

Drugstores (ドラッグストア)

There is a Satudora (サツドラ) near the Fukuharamashuten supermarket (9am-9pm).

Recommended cheap accommodation

Tabibitoyado Shoei (旅人宿昭栄)
Based in a little old school, this hostel is super friendly and a great place to meet fellow travelers. Highly recommended. *Beds from 1300 yen •* http://shoei-rider.hatenablog.com/ *(use Google Translate to book on their site, or use Booking.com)*

Mashuko Youth Hostel (摩周湖ユースホステル)
Big hostel with large kitchen and lounge, plus a large bath to relax in. Note the buses from Mashu station to the lake also stop off here. *Dorm beds from 2300 yen • Tel: 015-482-3098 •* http://www.youthhostel.or.jp/mashu/booking.htm

Hotel Masyu (ホテル摩周)
Private rooms and traditional 'teishoku' meals are available at this old fashioned Japanese hotel. *Room from 4000 yen • Tel: 015-482-2141 •* http://www.hotel-masyu.com/

Sakuragaoka Forest Park Auto Camping Ground (桜ヶ丘森林公園オートキャンプ場)
Large campsite with basic facilities. Book at an information center before if you can. *Campsites from 540 yen • Tel: 015-482-1491 • Mapcode: 462 819 167*36*

How to get there and away

By train
Trains are infrequent, so check times at Hyperdia.com. From Kushiro, take a train to Mashu station (76 mins, 1640 yen). There are also trains from Kawayu Onsen (16 mins, 360 yen).

By car or motorbike
Mashu station is about one hour and a half from Kushiro, and 20 minutes from Kawayu Onsen. *Useful Michi-no-eki roadside station: Just outside town at Mapcode 462 849 665, tel. 015-482-2500*

Mapcode: 462 851 154*55 (Mashu station)

Tourist information

There is an information center in Mashu station (9am-5pm), which also has wifi.

Kawayu Onsen (川湯温泉)

Walking down the moss-laden trails from Kawayu Onsen to the Tsutsujigahara Nature Trail

Kawayu Onsen is a small hot spring town north of Lake Mashu. Getting there is half the fun, with a walking route from the train station taking visitors via Iozan, an active volcano with sulfurous vents shooting out their yellow steam. Visitors can get up close too, if they so desire. The town itself is known for its especially acidic hot spring water, which can be experienced at a few free hot baths and by heading for a day visit at one of the local hotels.

Things to do

Walk from or to the station via Iozan (硫黄山)

The following are in order from the town of Kawayu Onsen to Kawayu Onsen station, but could easily be done the other way around. Some trail starts are tricky to find and may just be in Japanese, so if you need help show someone the Japanese names for the walks and they'll be able to show you where to go. There are also buses into and back from the town.

Tsutsujigahara Nature Trail (つつじヶ原自然探勝路)

An amazing trail near the foot of Iozan (Mount Io). Featuring miles of Japanese stone pine and Labrador tea plants over the mountain's lowlands, it's much more scenic than a bus of car ride. At the end you'll be greeted by the Iozan, so make sure you get up close to it for some sweet pictures of all that volcanic action. This trail connects up with the Aoba Tunnel trail. *Difficulty: Easy • Time required: About 1 hour • Starts from Kawayu Eco Museum Center's parking lot, finishes at the Mount Io parking lot*

Aoba Tunnel Nature Trail (青葉トンネル)

Heading through the deep forest between the station and town, this trail is a perfect way to escape the crowds and spend a bit of peaceful time to yourself. *Difficulty: Easy • Time required: About 45 minutes • Starts from the Mount Io parking lot (look for sign with Japanese name on it), finishes at Kawayu Onsen station via the highway (Route 391)*

Kawayu Onsen

Foot bath (川湯温泉足湯)

OK, so it's yet another hot spring foot bath, but this one is possibly the best. Surrounded by flowing streams of onsen water under a traditional Japanese roof, it's a very cool experience indeed. *FREE • 24h • Near the Kawayu Eco Museum Center*

Sakhalin Spruce Forest Trails (アカエゾマツの森)

Enter the peaceful pristine forest via these two trails from town. The volcanic ash from Mount Mashu and Mount Io is said to have made the plant life here grow slower than normal, which has left a rather different scenery from your standard forest. *Difficulty: Easy • Time required: 30 mins for short trail, 1 hour for long trail • Starts from Kawayu Eco Museum Center*

Taiho Sumo Museum (大鵬相撲記念館)

Dedicated to Taiho Toki, a local boy who became a sumo star in the 1960s. Achieving the highest title at the young age of 21, he still holds the record for most tournament victories. This museum shows off some of his greatest battles, but is lacking in English explanations. Not an essential visit, but an excellent rainy day location. *Adults 420 yen, children 200 yen• 5:30am-9pm • Near to the Seicomart convenience store*

Kitafukurou (きたふくろう)

A few locals told us this was the best hot spring in town for day trips and we certainly weren't disappointed. Small, yet uncrowded and with a lovely view of the forest outside, it sure made us feel relaxed after bathing here. Also has a free foot bath outside. *Adults 800 yen, children 400 yen • 12pm-8pm • Five minute walk from the town center, see map*

Public Bath (公衆浴場)

Need an even cheaper hot spring experience? The public bath is hardly the Ritz, but it uses the same water as elsewhere. *250 yen • 9am-8pm (closed Wednesdays) • Near to the post office in town*

Map of town center and station areas

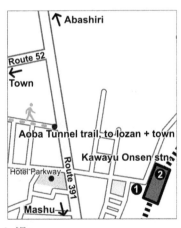

Kawayu Onsen Station Foot Bath (川湯温泉駅のあし湯)

Basic, and very hot, foot bath in the station building and the perfect place to hang out while you wait for your train. *FREE • 24h • Kawayu Onsen station*

Budget food

1) PANAPANA - Sweet little bakery. *Breads from 160 yen • 10am-7pm (closed Tuesdays and Wednesdays) • Just outside Kawayu Onsen station*

2) Orchard Grass (オーチャードグラス) - Japanese twists on western food. *Meals from 950 yen • 10am-5pm (closed Tuesdays) • Inside the Kawayu Onsen station building*

3) Otafuku Shokudo (お多福食堂) - Traditional noodle joint, with a variety of ramen, udon and soba bowls. *Meals from 680 yen • 11am-8pm • Town center, see map*

Iozan Visitor Center (硫黄山レストハウス) - No-frills ramen, curry and other Japanese staples. *Snacks from 300 yen, meals from 750 yen • 8am-5:30pm • Mount Io parking lot*

Cheap supermarkets (スーパー)

While there is no supermarket in town, there is a Seicomart convenience store (6am-12am) that has hot food and microwavable items.

Recommended cheap accommodation

Meitonomori Hotel Kitafukuro (名湯の森ホテルきたふくろう)

Big hotel in the center of town, with free wifi and its own hot spring. Prices are excellent considering you get your own Japanese style room with tatami mats. *Rooms from 6000 yen • Tel: 015-483-2960 • Reserve at Booking.com*

Kussharo-Genya Youth Guest House (屈斜路原野ユースゲストハウス)

Loads of different types of rooms are available at this recently refurbished hostel. *Dorm beds from 3000 yen, private rooms from 4200 yen • Tel: 015-484-2609 •* http://www.gogogenya.com/

How to get there and away

By train

Trains take you as far as Kawayu Onsen station, where you'll either need to walk or get a bus to the actual town itself. There are infrequent trains from Mashu station (16 mins, 360 yen) and Abashiri (2 hours, 1640 yen). Always check Hyperdia.com and make sure you are on the correct platform when returning (the train just went past when we were on the wrong one!).

By bus

If the trains aren't convenient, you can take a bus from Mashu station, with departures at 1:03pm, 4:03pm and 6:48pm and, for some reason, returning at 7:25am, 9:25am and 11am (37 mins, 560 yen). From Kawayu Onsen station to the town buses are timed with train departures and arrivals. There are buses at 8:25am, 10:35am, 12:05pm, 3:55pm, 5:05pm and 5:45pm (25 mins, 290 yen). They then return from the Kawayu Eco Museum Center at 8am, 10:05am, 11:35am, 3:25pm, 4:35pm, 5:15pm and 5:55pm. More buses are occasionally in operation, so confirm at your accommodation before.

By car or motorbike

The town is 20 minutes from Mashu and one hour from Abashiri. *Useful Michi-no-eki roadside station: Going north, there is one near Sattsuru station at Mapcode 444 439 466, tel. 0152-26-2288*

Mapcode: 731 802 149*58 (town center), 731 715 612*77 (Kawayu Onsen station)

Tourist information

The station has wifi and a map. In the town itself, the Hot Spring Information Centre also has wifi and brochures, but is unfortunately not always manned by English speakers (9am-5pm).

Shiretoko National Park and north-east Hokkaido

Shiretoko National Park (知床国立公園)

Added as a World Heritage Site in 2005, Shiretoko is one of Japan's best national parks. With roads going only about three quarters of the way up the peninsula, it offers unspoiled beauty and tranquility. The rest can be explored on foot or via cruises that depart from the main town of Utoro. You'll hope to see deer, foxes and, hopefully from the safety of a boat, brown bears.

Things to do

Most people will start at Shari, home of Shiretoko Shari station if coming on the train. From here you'll travel east into Shiretoko National Park.

Oshinkoshin Falls (オシンコシンの滝)

Part of Japan's official top 100 waterfalls list, this grand waterfall is a spectacular sight. There is a viewing platform about halfway to the top, leaving visitors just meters away from the water. *FREE • 24h • Located on the road between Shari and Utoro (free parking available). Buses on this route will make a brief stop here • Mapcode: 894 727 261*11*

Utoro (ウトロ)

The biggest settlement on the peninsular, Utoro is the main transportation hub and the departure point for the sightseeing cruises. It's still a small town in comparison to most in Japan, feeling rather laid back. The main distinctive feature of the town, though, is the many large rocks dotted across the place. Head up Oronko Rock (オロンコ岩) for a view over the town and port. *See 'How to get there and away' for bus instructions • Mapcode: 894 824 880*41*

Sightseeing cruises

Most tours depart from Utoro and head up the peninsular, taking visitors to spots that would take days to walk to, or are totally unreachable on land. Depending on the company and tour, they will either go halfway up the peninsular or right to the end, so you can decide at the boat terminal based on your budget and how much time you have. Along the way keep an eye out for brown bears strolling along the coastline, as well as whales, dolphins and sea lions. *Tours 3100-6500 yen • Cruises operate mid-April to mid-November • The port is located behind Oronko Rock in Utoro • Tel: 0152-24-2147 • Mapcode: 894 854 404*30 •* https://ms-aurora.com/shiretoko/

Furepe Waterfall (フレペの滝)

Fed by groundwater, meaning there is no visible river leading into it, Furepe Waterfall drops down a sheer cliff into the Sea of Okhotsk. From the Shiretoko Natural Center it's an easy 30 minute walk along a nature trail through the forest, then some grasslands, before ending up at an observation platform with views of the waterfall. Note you'll also get a glimpse of it on the sightseeing boat tours from Utoro. *The Shiretoko Nature Center is only several minutes down Route 334 from Utoro • Tel: 0152-24-2114 • Mapcode: 757 603 607*03*

Shiretoko Five Lakes (知床五湖)

Formed hundreds of years ago by the volcanic eruptions of Mount Io and others, these lakes are said to look like the five fingertips of god. The views they offer are just mind-blowing, surrounded by the wilderness of this huge forested park. There is an 800-meter elevated boardwalk that visitors can take from the parking lot to the first lake (open late April to late November). It is also possible to go on a longer walk into the park, but there are limits on the number of walkers, lectures that need to be attended and other rules depending on the time of year. Visit https://www.goko.go.jp/multilingual_eng/ for this year's dates and to sign up. *See 'How to get there and away' for bus instructions • Tel: 0152-24-3323 • Mapcode: 757 730 274*03*

Budget food

There is a 7-Eleven and Seicomart convenience store on Route 334 just before you turn into the sightseeing cruise port. The Michi-no-eki in Utoro also has a restaurant (9am-6:30pm).

Recommended cheap accommodation

Shiretoko Hostel Hanare (知床ホステルハナレ)

Free wifi, private parking, its own hot spring and a super cozy atmosphere at the top of a hill in Utoro. *Beds from 3950 yen • Tel: 0152-24-2124•* https://www.shiretoko-guesthouse.com/lg_en/

How to get there and away

By bus

Shari Bus run very infrequent buses from Shiretoko Shari station to the Shiretoko Nature Center (70 mins, 1800 yen), stopping off along the way in Utoro. There are also buses to the five lakes from Utoro (25 minutes, 700 yen) and the station (90 mins, 2000 yen) in summer.

By car or motorbike

The main town, Utoro, is about one and a half hours from Abashiri and two hours from Kawayu Onsen. Outside of winter, tourists should definitely go via the Shiretoko Pass (知床峠), the road that connects Utoro and a town called Rausa on Route 334. Driving up to a high elevation closer to the mountain tops, you'll get superb views of Mount Rausa and Kunashiri Island to the east. The view is especially spectacular in autumn (usually best in early October). *Useful Michi-no-eki roadside station: There is one in Utoro at Mapcode 894 824 879, tel. 0152-22-5000*

Mapcode: 894 824 880*41 (tourist information center in Utoro)

Tourist information

There is one in Utoro, next to the above Michi-no-eki roadside station (8am-5:30pm).

Abashiri (網走)

Abashiri is the largest city north of Akan Mashu National Park and an interesting spot to drop in for a day. Most famous for its drift ice tours, the city also has some very notable museums to explore any time of the year.

Things to do

See the drift ice

The Sea of Okhotsk is the northern hemisphere's most southerly point to see drifting sea ice. As the ice does not always come up to the coast, taking a sightseeing cruise with Aurora Sightseeing Boats is recommended to get the fullest experience. The best time to see it is usually in the second half of February, but the season lasts from around late January to late March. *3300 yen (3000 yen tickets can be found at Japanican.com) • Various times throughout the day • Departs from Abashiri Port, a 10 minute walk or short bus ride from the bus terminal. Buses from the station also stop nearby (10 mins, 200 yen) • Tel: 0152-43-6000 • Mapcode: 305 678 309*88*

Abashiri Prison Museum (物館網走監獄)

An outdoor museum using the original buildings of the old Abashiri Prison. Used in the Meiji Period to vanish political prisoners away from the rest of the population, the huge complex tells the fascinating stories of the inmates' lives and what they had to go through every day. Visitors can enter the old buildings, such as the bath house, cells and a rather creepy punishment chamber. *Adults 1000 yen, children 540-750 yen (get online discounts at https://www.kangoku.jp/multilingual_english/) • May to September: 8:30am-6pm. October to April: 9am-5pm • Buses operate here from Abashiri station and the bus center every one or two hours (get off at the Hakubutsukan Abashiri Kangoku bus stop). Note that they do not operate during some weekends, so it would be best to walk or hitchhike in such a situation • Tel: 0152-45-2411 • Mapcode: 305 582 179*47*

Hokkaido Museum of Northern Peoples (北海道立北方民族博物)

The perfect place to come if you want to know more about the Ainu people, the indigenous peoples of Hokkaido. This museum explains all you'll need to know about their culture and everyday lives, as well as people in other parts of the world who live in similar northern climates. *Adults 550 yen, children 200 yen • July to September: 9am-5pm. October to June: 9:30am-*

4:30pm • Buses operate here from Abashiri station and the bus center every one or two hours (get off at Minzoku Hakubutsukan-mae bus stop). Note that they do not operate during some weekends, so it would be best to walk or hitchhike in such a situation • Tel: 0152-45-3888 • Mapcode: 305 584 277*82

Budget food

Abashiri is rather spread out, so it's best just to head to a convenience store to get food if you don't happen to see something good. There is a large supermarket called Food Master Basic opposite the public library over Abashiri River (9:30am-9pm, tel. 0152-61-6555).

Recommended cheap accommodation

Abashiri Ryoho-no-Oka Youth Hostel (網走流氷の丘ユースホステル)
A little out of town, this hostel is in a great location looking over the Sea of Okhotsk. Excellent kitchen facilities, plus you can add on cheap breakfasts and/or dinner. *Dorm beds from 3250 yen* • *Tel: 0152-43-8558* • http://www.jyh.or.jp

Toyoko Inn (東横イン)
No-frills, low-cost hotel right across the road from the station. *Rooms from 6500 yen* • *Tel: 0152-45-1043* • https://www.toyoko-inn.com

How to get there and away

By air
Memanbetsu Airport is a convenient way to get to Abashiri or away. Shuttle buses timed with flight departures and arrivals connect the airport with Abashiri (25 mins, 880 yen).

By train
There are infrequent trains from Kawayu Onsen (2 hours, 1640 yen) and some comfy Limited Express trains from Asahikawa (4 hours, 7450 yen)

By bus
There are buses every hour or two from Sapporo station, including a night bus if you want to cut out the cost of accommodation for the night (6 hours, 6390 yen). There are also buses that depart at 7:30am from Sounkyo Onsen (5 hours, 5000 yen), which need to be booked at least two days in advance. This can be done via most bus centers or tourist information centers.

By car or motorbike
Abashiri is one hour from Kawayu Onsen and three hours from Asahikawa. Parking is available at the boat terminal and at the museums. *Useful Michi-no-eki roadside station: Inside the boat terminal*

Mapcode: 305 676 090*58 (Abashiri station)

Tourist information

In Abashiri station (weekdays 12pm-5pm, weekends 9am-5pm) and in the sightseeing boat terminal (9am-6pm).

Japanese for budget travelers

Essential phrases

Do you speak English? - Eigo ga hanasemas ka? / 英語が話せますか？
Hello! - Konnichiwa! / こんにちは！
Yes - Hai / はい
No - Iie / いいえ
Thank you - Arigatou / ありがとう
Sorry - Sumimasen / すみません
I don't understand - Wakarimasen / わかりません
Please write down (e.g. number, price) - Kaite kudasai / かいてください
Where is the _? - _ wa doko des ka? / _はどこですか？

Insert the following above to ask for directions:
Toilet = Toire / トイレ • Train station = Eki / えき • Gas station = Gasusutando / ガススタンド

Shopping

How much is this? - Ikura des ka? / いくらですか？
Do you have _? - _ arimas ka? / _ありますか？

Getting food and drink

Do you have an English menu? - Eigo no menyu wa arimas ka? / 英語のメニューはありますか？
I'd like _ please - _ o kudasai / _をください
That please - Kore o kudasai / これをください (point at the item)
Water please (save on drinks) - Omizu o kudasai / お水をください
Refill please! (use if free refills available) - Okawari! / おかわり！
Takeout please - Teiku-auto de / テイクアウトで
Eat-in please - Eeto-in de / イートインで
Is there a cover or table charge? - Chaaji arimas ka? / チャージありますか？

Traveling around

Please tell me when we get to _. (good for buses/trains with no English signs) - _ ni tsuku toki ni oshiete kudasai / _に着くときに教えてください

Numbers

0 - zero / 〇
1 - ichi / 一
2 - ni / 二
3 - san / 三
4 - shi/yon / 四
5 - go / 五
6 - roku / 六
7 - shichi/nana / 七
8 - hatchi / 八
9 - kyū / 九
10 - jū / 十
11 - jū-ichi (sound for 10, then sound for 1) / 十一 (so 12 is 'jū-ni', 13 is 'jū-san' etc)
20 - ni-jū (sound for 2, then sound for 10) / 二十 (so 30 is 'san-jū', 31 is 'san-jū-ichi' etc)

Many thanks for reading

Help spread the word!

Please help the book by writing a review on the website where you bought the book, sharing the book on Facebook, Twitter or Instagram, or telling a friend. As this is a self-funded indie project, it would be super useful and very much appreciated! It will also allow me to continue to write more budget travel books about this amazing country. Doumo arigatou!

Like or follow us to get the latest tips and deals

Join or follow Super Cheap Guides to get the latest information on new discounts, deals and cherry blossom forecasts, plus interesting budget travel reports. You can also head to our website to read all the latest information or get it sent straight to your inbox by joining the newsletter.

Website: https://www.supercheapguides.com/
Facebook: facebook.com/supercheapguides
Instagram: @SuperCheapGuides
Twitter: @SuperCheapGuide

About the Author

Super Cheap Hokkaido was written by Matthew Baxter, a British travel author who has lived in and out of Japan for many years. Having traveled across the country for more than a decade, without much money, he has built up an extensive knowledge of budget travel in the Land of the Rising Sun. He now writes professionally for several websites and publications, such as the Japan National Tourist Association, Japan Visitor and All About Japan.

You can contact the author via matt@supercheapguides.com

Picture Attribution

Also available from Super Cheap Guides

 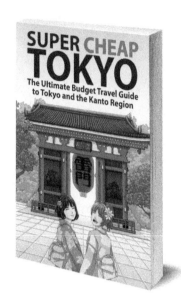

Super Cheap Japan: Budget Travel in Tokyo, Kyoto, Osaka, Nara, Hiroshima and Surrounding Areas (ISBN: 978-1-9998100-0-9)
The ultimate budget travel guide to a cheap holiday in Honshu (Japan's main island). Go shopping for $4 clothes in Tokyo, enjoy inexpensive hikes in Nikko, or visit Kyoto's beautiful shrines and gardens on the cheap; all with this super helpful guide.

Super Cheap Tokyo: The Ultimate Budget Travel Guide to Tokyo and the Kanto Region (ISBN: 978-1-9998100-5-4)
Super Cheap Tokyo is all you'll need for budget holiday in Tokyo and the surrounding Kanto region. Buy clothes in fashion heaven Harajuku for under $10, spend next to nothing on a day's hiking or relax in a free Japanese garden; it's all here in this easy-to-use travel guide.

Check out https://www.supercheapguides.com/ for more information!

CPSIA information can be obtained
at www.ICGtesting.com
Printed in the USA
LVHW082147270120
645014LV00008B/509